SPIR
I

TO

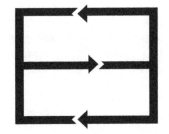

ROB HOWARD

Cover and interior design by Kirsten Howard

Second Edition

ISBN 9781694979902

CONTENTS

For my family
and our face-to-face relationships.

FOREWORD

This book is not for everyone. It's for a person who, for lack of a better term, is "stuck." I could say it another way. It is for the person who is not experiencing their life with God in ways they would like and expect. Maybe I should say it is for the person who is "thirsty."

I say this because of the tried and true adage ... "you can lead a horse to water, but you can't make him drink." I wouldn't be writing this foreword if I did not believe what Rob writes is water for your soul. But Rob didn't write this to be read, but to be experienced. His invitation is about using some tools that can help you get unstuck.

And I believe he is the right person to get you going. Rob and I began working together at Fellowship Bible Church about 15 years ago. During the week, and many weekends we crossed paths in the hallway, sat across the table in meetings, and went deep one on one. He has reported to me, and, I have reported to him. Together, we have facilitated multiple leader development cohorts which required both of us to put down the "mask" and bring our "true self" to the table.

As I watched Rob invite God to commune with the truest part himself (often the parts you don't want anyone to know or see), I watched God change him. And so did others. Little did I know he was creating many of the exercises you hold in your hand during those days and working through them on his own to grow a relationship with God that is face to face.

It seems those closest to us, day in and day out, rarely notice the changes we are going through. It often takes the "absent uncle" who after years of not seeing you declares, "I can't believe how much you have grown! It was just yesterday you were riding a tricycle!!"

Well, I'm no absent uncle. I've watched Rob for 15 years. And I can't believe how much he has grown. He is not who he once was. He's not yet all he will be. And, he is not stuck. You won't be either ... if you are willing to accept his invitations.

Lloyd Shadrach
Teaching Pastor, Fellowship Bible Church
Brentwood and Franklin, TN

INTRODUCTION

There is a language I didn't begin to speak until much later in my life—the language of being. Several years ago I was asked to describe what it's like for me to be with God, so I listed off the many things I did for Him. I didn't squirm. My relationship with God is real, my prayer life matters, and all my doing was my reality. I am a doer. I naturally get things done and work hard. I love to make lists and check them off (which is the reason you make a list). A friend once told me that what I considered my good midwestern work ethic was really called workaholism. I didn't know what to do with that.

ISN'T HARD WORK A GOOD THING?

It is. There is gold in all the hard work, there is also shadow. When the hard work becomes my identity, when it doesn't flow from a deep well of connection with Christ, then it is unhealthy, it is shadow. What I began to unpack over the course of the next year, is that for me to "be" with God in relationship meant we would "do" things together ... my full-time job in ministry, up early on Sundays, staying late for meetings, taking on more than what God had called me to do. Being with God meant doing things for Him or with Him. I had a side-by-side relationship with God.

WHAT WOULD IT LOOK LIKE TO HAVE A FACE-TO-FACE RELATIONSHIP WITH GOD?

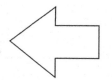

I began to read a lot of books. With a group of men, I was learning more and more about my false self (what I wanted others to see—projection—my hard work and success) and my true self (my identity as a child of God, my character, and my vulnerable, honest self). It was as if I looked at life, at others from behind the mask of what I wanted them to see—how I wanted them to see me. As I became more aware of that mask, I realized I also held it up to God. I read in *The Return of the Prodigal Son* by Henri Nouwen, "The question is not 'How am I to find God?' but 'How am I let to let myself be found by Him?' The question is not 'How am I to know God?' but 'How am I to let myself be known by Him?' And finally, the question is not 'How do I love God?' but 'How am I to let myself be loved by God?'" There was a relief I felt deep within me that I could not explain. I had to keep digging deeper.

WHO AM I WITHOUT ALL THE GOOD I DO?

During this time there was a growing awareness of what was going on in me—not just what I was thinking, but also my emotions and my desires. I realized I struggled being present in my day—in meetings, in conversations with my children, my wife, even with God. I was so busy, I had so much to get done. I remember describing the feeling as "having a large piece of the sky that I need to hold up." Responsibility. Duty. Those are extremely weighty words for me. There was always a list being made in my head, things to remember and write down, forecasting future problems to solve before they arrived. I could be on vacation with my family, yet in my thoughts I was working. I could sit and play with one of my children and my mind could be miles away.

A counselor and coach I worked with at the time brought the idea to me of the polarity loop. On one side is our "being" and the other our "doing." He suggested that my doing was way out of balance with my being. Jesus describes this in John 15 as He talks about the vine and the branches. Our doing should flow from our being—our abiding in the vine. It's like breathing in and breathing out. If we attempt to hold our breath, at some point something's got to give. My unhealthy balance of doing wore me out, something gave. That was the burnout I'd already experienced in my life and could see coming again if something didn't change. I needed to grow in what it meant for me to be with God, to allow my doing to flow from a healthier place.

As I grew in my awareness of what was going on within me, I began to work at being present in the moment. The first step for me on that journey was awareness. My awareness led to greater presence. As I learned to be present with God I began to experience what it's like to simply be with God. And as my being with God has grown, those moments have become sacred.

AWARENESS
IS THE KEY
THAT OPENS UP
THE SACRAMENT
OF THE
PRESENT MOMENT.
WHEN WE CONSCIOUSLY
TAKE THIS KEY
AND TURN THE LOCK
ON THE
HERE AND NOW,
THE PRESENT MOMENT
OPENS UP INTO
A BANQUET WHERE
THE DIVINE PRESENCE
SURROUNDS US
LIKE THE AIR
WE BREATHE.

Albert Haase, *Coming Home to Your True Self*

I studied Spiritual Direction with the Institute for Christian Spirituality at Lipscomb University. Spiritual Direction is helping someone tend to their relationship with God and respond to their awareness of God in everyday life. I learned with a Cohort of nine people over the course of two years. We read countless books, practiced and received Spiritual Direction, discussed and questioned our material, learned to be curious and ask good, open-ended questions, and began to understand and grow in experiencing the more contemplative spiritual practices.

> "SILENCE IS NOT ABSENCE BUT PRESENCE. LIKE ELIJAH IN THE CAVE I FIND THAT GOD IS HERE IN 'THE SOUND OF SHEER SILENCE' (TO USE THE WORDS OF A RECENT TRANSLATION) — GOD PRESENT IN THIS TOTAL STILLNESS. SILENCE AND STILLNESS ARE GIFTS WHICH ARE GENTLE, FRAGILE, TO BE HANDLED WITH CARE, ABOVE ALL IN ALLOWING TIME TO WAIT AND TO LISTEN."

-Esther De Waal, *Lost in Wonder*

"Silence and stillness" has taken a lot of practice. Our culture is busy, striving, loud, and hectic. There is always noise, work, traffic, meetings, and entertainment. My inner world reflected my external world for so long. It takes me quite some time to still all that is churning within me. I have to linger for a while, slowing down, stilling my thoughts, before I feel I am able to be fully present with God, able to let go of distractions. I've gotten used to early mornings (which I never thought I'd do), in my office alone in the silence, with a regular pattern to my prayer time and journaling …

**HOW DO I COME TO THIS PRAYER TIME?
WHAT DO I DESIRE FROM GOD DURING THIS TIME?
WHAT RESONATES WITHIN ME
AS I READ THE PASSAGE?
HOW DO I ENGAGE WITH GOD ABOUT IT?**

My relationship with God grew as I learned to sit face to face with God—fully known, honest, vulnerable, letting Him love the me behind the mask of my false self. I was able to invite Jesus into my most vulnerable places—my failures not just my successes, my fears not just my confidence, my deepest idols not just my surface sin.

"HONESTY BEFORE GOD
IS NOT SIMPLY AVOIDING LIES.
IT IS BRINGING OUR FULL SELF TO GOD. RATHER THAN
TRYING TO FIX THINGS UP BEFORE TURNING TO GOD,
GENUINE PRAYER IS TURNING TO GOD IN THE MIDST OF
THE MESS THAT IS THE REALITY OF OUR INNER WORLD.
IT IS TURNING TO GOD IN THE MIDST OF OUR
CONFUSION AND DOUBT
OUR ANGER
OUR HOPES
OUR FEARS
OUR FANTASIES
OUR PAIN
OUR COPING
OUR DEFENSES
OUR STRUGGLES
OUR SIN
AND OUR BROKENNESS
THERE IS NO CURE FOR THAT WHICH MOST DEEPLY AILS US
UNLESS WE COME TO GOD WITH NOTHING HELD BACK."

Dr. David Benner, *Opening to God*

The more I invited Jesus into those dark places, the more grace I felt—not just knew at a cognitive level but experienced at the depths of who I am. The more honest I became with God, the more honest I became with myself and with others. My prayer time with God in the Bible had always felt like duty, it was becoming my desire, my delight. Over time, as I sat face to face with God, I began to see more clearly my true self—my identity as a child of God—and became more comfortable letting go of the false identity I'd projected for so long.

> ❝ **NEARLY ALL THE WISDOM WHICH WE POSSESS, THAT IS TO SAY, TRUE AND SOUND WISDOM, CONSISTS OF TWO PARTS:**
>
> # THE KNOWLEDGE OF GOD AND OF OURSELVES.
>
> **BUT, WHILE JOINED BY MANY BONDS, WHICH ONE PRECEDES AND BRINGS FORTH THE OTHER IS NOT EASY TO DISCERN.** ❞

John Calvin, *Institutes of the Christian Religion*

I spent the better part of this past year reading through the Psalms, coming to God with nothing held back, learning to speak with Him as the psalmists did. I feel like I read the Psalms as John Steinbeck describes Tom from his novel *East of Eden*, "Samuel rode lightly on top of a book and he balanced happily among ideas the way a man rides white rapids in a canoe. But Tom got into a book, crawled and groveled between the covers, tunneled like a mole among the thoughts, and came up with the book all over his face and hands."

The Spiritual Exercises that follow have come from my personal prayer time in the Psalms. They flow from my face-to-face time with God … my wrestle with what was going on in my life as I engaged the Scripture and brought the dark places, my fears and anxiety, loneliness, the excitement, gratitude … everything I felt and desired to Jesus. They are made up of the questions I asked myself as I wrote down what resonated with me in the passage. And they come from my personal dialog with God as I engaged Him in every aspect of my life, and He drew me deeper and deeper.

"TO SEEK GOD'S FACE IS NOT TO FIND SOME PLACE IN SPACE WHERE GOD IS LOCATED. RATHER, IT IS TO HAVE OUR HEARTS ENABLED BY THE HOLY SPIRIT TO SENSE HIS REALITY AND PRESENCE. 'THE LORD SPOKE TO YOU FACE TO FACE OUT OF THE FIRE ON THE MOUNTAIN' (DEUT 5:4; CF. GEN 32:30; NUM 6:25-26). PEOPLE ARE CALLED BY GOD TO 'PRAY AND SEEK MY FACE' (2 CHRON 7:14). TO LOSE A SENSE OF GOD'S PRESENCE IS TO LOSE GOD'S FACE (PS 13:1), AND TO SEEK HIS FACE IS TO SEEK COMMUNION WITH HIM, A REAL INTERACTION WITH GOD, SHARING THOUGHTS AND LOVE."

Tim Keller, *Prayer*

I encourage you to dig deep in the Psalms. Wrestle with God about His Word, what's going on in your heart, and what challenges lie before you. Mark up your Bible with your thoughts, questions, joys, sorrows, and deepest desires. Engage God in your journal. If you don't have a regular pattern of sitting with God, try the four questions I mentioned earlier. That is how I begin every prayer time in my journal.

> **JOURNAL KEEPING IS A HIGHLY INTENTIONAL REFLECTION ON THE EVENTS OF OUR DAYS. IT DIFFERS FROM A DIARY BY ITS FOCUS ON WHY AND WHEREFORE RATHER THAN WHO AND WHAT. THE EXTERNAL EVENTS ARE SPRINGBOARDS FOR UNDERSTANDING THE DEEPER WORKINGS OF GOD IN THE HEART.**

Richard Foster, *Prayer*

My desire has been to collect these Spiritual Exercises for you to use in your personal prayer time or in a small group setting. I hope they can be used to deepen your face-to-face relationship with God, or to begin to experience a face-to-face relationship with Him. I pray they increase your awareness, which leads you to greater presence, ultimately to sacred being with God.

> **"ABIDE IN ME,**
> **AND I IN YOU.**
> **AS THE BRANCH CANNOT BEAR FRUIT BY ITSELF,**
> **UNLESS IT ABIDES IN THE VINE,**
> **NEITHER CAN YOU, UNLESS YOU ABIDE IN ME.**
> **I AM THE VINE;**
> **YOU ARE THE BRANCHES. WHOEVER ABIDES IN ME AND I IN HIM, HE IT IS THAT BEARS MUCH FRUIT, FOR APART FROM ME YOU CAN DO NOTHING."**
> John 15:4-5

" MORE AND MORE
IS THE CONVICTION FORCED
UPON MY HEART THAT EVERY MAN
MUST TRAVERSE THE
TERRITORY OF THE PSALMS HIMSELF
IF HE WOULD KNOW WHAT
A GOODLY LAND THEY ARE.
THEY FLOW WITH MILK AND HONEY,
BUT NOT TO STRANGERS;
THEY ARE ONLY FERTILE TO LOVERS
OF THEIR HILLS AND VALES.
NONE BUT THE HOLY SPIRIT CAN GIVE A MAN
THE KEY TO THE TREASURY OF DAVID;
AND EVEN HE GIVES IT RATHER TO
EXPERIENCE THAN STUDY.
HAPPY HE WHO FOR HIMSELF
KNOWS THE
SECRET OF THE PSALMS. "

Charles Spurgeon, *Treasury of David*

MEDITATING ON GOD'S WORD

⟶

[PSALM 1]

I've struggled with God's Word. I want to love it and delight in it, but I've felt the duty and responsibility of it with my role in full-time ministry. I wasn't surprised as I read Psalm 1, that what resonated with me was, "and on his law he meditates day and night," and then the metaphor, "He is like a tree planted by streams of water."

I began to write in my journal about some of my struggle with God's Word ... the responsibility I feel, the pressure I've put on myself, the burnout I referred to in the Introduction from over-working things, and being disconnected from God ... my abiding in the vine. I imagined myself as the tree the psalmist speaks of and saw myself walking around on my roots, trying with good intention to hand out all the fruit I have, polish it up for presentation, unaware that I've left the stream of living water that feeds my root system.

As I've wrestled with "duty and delight" I've come to realize that duty equals law, and delight equals grace. There were so many expectations I was putting on myself, God's Word, and God Himself. There was a reality—my reality—I didn't know how to face or name. I understood the importance of knowing the Word, understanding it with clear theology, but didn't know how to allow the Word to flow through the deepest parts of me and affect my emotions and the longings of my heart. Reading Scripture differently—meditatively—has allowed me to engage not only my mind, but my heart and my will as well.

Richard Foster wrote in his book *Prayer*, "In the meditation upon Scripture we cannot, for example, read the story of God's word to Abraham to sacrifice his son Isaac in total detachment, thankful that we are not in his shoes. We are, in point of face, in his shoes! Along with Abraham we, too, struggle with the decision to sacrifice the one thing most precious to us. As Abraham did, so we are brought to the place of giving over to God our most cherished possession. And, like Abraham, we come down from the mountain with the meaning of the words my and *mine* forever changed."

This is the way I've attempted to read the Psalms—not in detachment, glad I wasn't being chased by armies and hiding in caves—but with my heart open to the leading of the Holy Spirit, asking myself what I am running from or running to, naming the usual foes that wage war against my soul, asking God to face them with me.

I want to be clear, in meditating on God's Word we aren't attempting to make it mean what we want it to mean. We are asking the Holy Spirit to help us get the Word from our mind to the deepest parts of us—to ask what it means for us and for all we're facing today. Tim Keller writes in his book *Prayer*, "Meditation on a text of the Bible assumes that, through study and interpretation, you already know something about what the text means. You can't reflect on or enjoy what you don't understand."

As you engage the Psalms, get a good Study Bible or commentary. It is important to understand the original author's intent and how the passage fits into the whole story of the Bible. Read and reread the Scripture. Memorize it. Read it aloud. Rewrite it in your journal. And as you engage in your day, I pray your actions flow from your delight and meditation in God's Word.

> JUST AS YOU DO NOT ANALYZE THE WORDS
> OF SOMEONE YOU LOVE,
> BUT ACCEPT THEM AS THEY ARE SAID TO YOU,
> ACCEPT THE WORD OF SCRIPTURE AND PONDER
> IT IN YOUR HEART, AS MARY DID.
> THAT IS ALL. THAT IS MEDITATION.

Dietrich Bonhoeffer, *The Way to Freedom.*

[PSALM 1]

SPIRITUAL EXERCISE

---

1. Begin with a few minutes of silence and let your heart be still.

2. Two questions to answer before engaging the Word ...

   • How do you come to this prayer time? "I come today ..."
   • What do you desire from God during this time? "I desire ..."

3. Read through Psalm 1, slowly. I encourage you to read it through a few times, read it aloud, even rewrite it in your journal. What stands out to you? Write it down.

4. To engage the psalm, we'll use questions from Tim Keller's book *Prayer* from his chapter "As Conversation: Meditating on His Word." Ask the Holy Spirit to lead you as you work through these questions. You might choose two or three, or work through all five.

   • How am I living in light of this?
   • What difference does this make?
   • Am I taking this seriously?
   • If I believed and held to this, how would that change things?
   • When I forget this, how does that affect me and all my relationships?

5. Two final questions ...

   • What desires or deep longings of your heart does this make you aware of?

   • What might God's invitation be to you in this place?

6. Close your time with a prayer to God, responding to how you experienced Him through Psalm 1.

7. If you're working through this exercise in a group, share what you feel comfortable sharing.

A WHOLEHEARTED APPROACH TO A CHALLENGE

[PSALM 8]

Our church has taken the past year to reimagine our mission and vision. The meetings for us, with a few consultants, have been exhausting and we did not leave any stones unturned. The result has been what we hoped—clarity, unity, and strong movement forward. We have been strong on the heart ... bringing our whole heart, our whole self, to our relationship with God and others. We describe being a wholehearted follower in this way ...

The Problem of a Divided Heart

In the Bible, the word "heart" is used to describe the core, or control center, of a person. The heart includes your thoughts, emotions, desires, and choices. While made to function as an integrated and connected whole, in humanity's fall, our hearts became fragmented, disintegrated, separated, and divided. As a result, all of our relationships are marked by brokenness—our relationship with God, with other people, with creation, and even with ourselves. (Genesis 1-3)

What Is Wholehearted Life in Jesus?

Wholehearted life in Jesus is the lifelong process of our thoughts, emotions, desires, and choices uniting through the cross to find our deepest longings and greatest hopes satisfied in Jesus alone (Psalm 86:11). This kind of life is expressed through four characteristics ... Renewed Mind, Healthy Relationships, Satisfied Soul, and Active Faith.

What we will do in this exercise is explore the whole person —our thoughts, emotions, desires, and choices—as we engage a challenge we're facing. In the diagram below, notice we don't get to choices without going back through the "cross" at the center, allowing the gospel to influence everything. I think of it like this ... once we have greater clarity around what we're thinking, feeling, and our deepest desires, then we invite Jesus into the midst of that to help us choose how to act. We'll do this by engaging a psalm. It is important in this process to engage all four areas of the heart— instead of the habits we can be used to like "thinking what to do then choosing to act," or "feeling a strong emotion and choosing to react." This exercise is one that can be applied to many psalms. We'll ground ourselves in Psalm 8 for now.

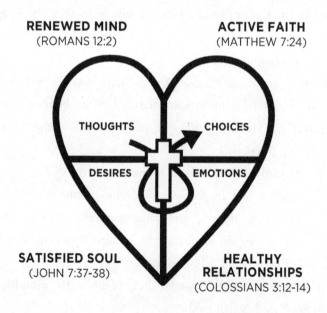

RENEWED MIND
(ROMANS 12:2)

ACTIVE FAITH
(MATTHEW 7:24)

THOUGHTS

CHOICES

DESIRES

EMOTIONS

SATISFIED SOUL
(JOHN 7:37-38)

**HEALTHY
RELATIONSHIPS**
(COLOSSIANS 3:12-14)

[PSALM 8]
SPIRITUAL EXERCISE

1. Begin with a few minutes of silence and let your heart be still.

2. Think of a challenge you're facing—a relational or leadership challenge—and write it down in a sentence or two.

3. We'll engage three questions to start ...
    - What are your thoughts around this challenge?
      Apply reason to it, what you know, what is true.
    - What are you feeling regarding this challenge?
      Write down the emotions that you're aware of.
    - What deep desires resonate in you?
      What you long for and hope for.

4. Read through Psalm 8, slowly. Write down the words or phrases that stand out to you.

5. The final question ...
    - What choice do you need to make?

6. Close with a prayer, thanking God for His presence, asking Him for what you need in this place, and for the courage to follow His invitation to you.

7. If you're working through this exercise in a group, share what you feel comfortable sharing.

Most any psalm will work with this exercise, but here are a few others to consider:

Psalm 20 - Trust in the Name of the Lord our God

Psalm 23 - The Lord Is My Shepherd

Psalm 27 - The Lord Is My Light and My Salvation

Psalm 28 - The Lord Is My Strength and Shield

Psalm 40 - My Help and My Deliverer

Psalm 46 - God Is Our Fortress

[PSALM 9]

I mentioned in the Introduction that I have a simple routine I follow in my prayer time—four questions. I love routines. Everything in its proper order. Expectations met. I know that can get me in a rut, so I decided to take an approach to this psalm that is much different.

The following exercise is based on one I learned in my study of Spiritual Direction. I remembered it as I recently watched a TED Talk by Graham Shaw on "How to Remember More." He said, "If we take that information and turn it into a picture with a drawing, we remember it. Because when we draw we remember more." When I get out of my left brain—logic and linear thinking —and engage more of my right brain—imagination and creativity—my experience is much different. When I draw something the information that I know goes more deeply into my soul, to the deeper parts of who I am.

I encourage you to try and engage with God in a different way. See how His Spirit might lead as you take your journaling or usual routine and engage the more creative side of you. The goal is not a fantastic drawing, but to express what you're feeling and invite God into it.

[PSALM 9]

SPIRITUAL EXERCISE

---

1. Begin with a few minutes of silence and let your heart be still.

2. Read through Psalm 9, slowly.

3. Think of a recent experience that was moving or challenging. Journal about it by writing a paragraph or two.

4. Take that experience and condense it into two or three words.

5. Remembering the experience, how did it feel in your body?

6. Draw that feeling.
   (Colored pencils or markers could increase your creativity.)

7. Ask the Holy Spirit to lead you as you make some observations of your drawing.

8. Compare and contrast your image with your original paragraph and/or the two or three words. Write down what stands out to you.

9. Re-read Psalm 9:1-2, then verses 9-10.

10. Pray along the direction of ... Whether we're giving thanks in gladness as we remember God's wonderful deeds or holding on to Him tightly as our stronghold in times of trouble, in either situation He is present. We can rejoice. Finish your prayer by reading Psalm 9:11-14.

11. If you're working through this exercise in a group, share what you feel comfortable sharing.

WRITING YOUR
OWN LAMENT

→

[PSALM 13]

"How long, O Lord?" That's familiar language to me. How long? Why, God? Where are You? Many times my answer wouldn't come, God felt hidden, and I didn't know how much more I could take. The language is familiar, but it took me a while to own those thoughts and feelings fully with God. For years I tried to present my "best self" to God, for Him to be pleased with me. I've learned over time to present my most honest and vulnerable self to God, like I mentioned the Henri Nouwen quote in the Introduction ... myself fully found, fully known, and fully loved by Him.

As we've talked already about the idea of "wholehearted," that can help us with a language to bring before God. Referring to the diagram on page 28, it's not only what's "above the line" that matters—what we think and how we choose to act—but also what's below the line—our emotions and desires. Our emotions matter. We are made in God's image (Genesis 1:27), and our God is an emotional God ...

Ezekiel 5:13 "Thus shall my anger spend itself, and I will vent my fury upon them and satisfy myself. And they shall know that I am the Lord—that I have spoken in my jealousy —when I spend my fury upon them."

Jeremiah 32:41 "I will rejoice in doing them good, and I will plant them in this land in faithfulness, with all my heart and all my soul."

Psalm 103:13 "As a father shows compassion to his children, so the Lord shows compassion to those who fear Him."

The desires and deep longings of our heart matter. We are made in God's image, and our God is a God of deep desires ...

Jeremiah 24:7 "I will give them a heart to know that I am the Lord, and they shall be my people and I will be their God, for they shall return to me with their whole heart."

Hosea 6:6 "For I desire steadfast love and not sacrifice, the knowledge of God rather than burnt offerings."

Matthew 11:28-30 "Come to me, all who labor and are heavy laden, and I will give you rest. Take my yoke upon you, and learn from me, for I am gentle and lowly in heart, and you will find rest for your souls. For my yoke is easy, and my burden is light."

God longs for us to bring our deepest desires and strong, honest emotions to Him ... to express to Him our anger, hopelessness, loneliness, loss, pain, doubt, fear, and anxiety. I encourage you to let yourself be fully known and fully loved by God as you bring your lament to Him.

66

**THE PSALMS
ALLOW US TO LAMENT,**
TO CRY OUT IN PAIN AND ANGUISH.
BUT THEY ALSO EFFECT
A TRANSFORMATION.
AS WE PRAY OR SING, OR SHOUT THEM,
THE PSALMS USE THE STRONG LANGUAGE
WHICH DOES NOT TRY TO PRETEND
THAT WE ARE NICE.
SO WE CAN GROAN,
COMPLAIN BITTERLY,
TELL GOD HOW UNFAIR
HIS ACTIONS ARE, INDULGE IN BITTER GRIEF
AND REVEAL ALL OUR MENTAL HURTS
AND DESPAIR ...
EVEN THE SAYING OF THESE HATEFUL
THINGS OUT LOUD IS A WAY
OF ACKNOWLEDGING THEM,
AND OF TURNING
THEM OVER TO GOD.
IF WE KNOW THAT
WE ARE BEING LISTENED TO
BY THIS GOD
THEN WE ARE AT LEAST
**STANDING IN A PLACE WHERE
GOD'S HEALING CAN BEGIN.**

99

Esther De Waal, *Lost in Wonder*

[PSALM 13]

SPIRITUAL EXERCISE

1. Begin with a few minutes of silence and let your heart be still.

2. Read through Psalm 13, slowly.

3. Read through the psalm again and notice the three parts to the lament ...
   • Complaint (vs. 1-2)
   • Petition (vs. 3-4)
   • Praise (vs. 5-6)

4. Spend time thinking through how you're doing. Is there a difficult situation before you? Are you lonely, angry, or afraid? What in life feels overwhelming? Where are you carrying fear or anxiety? Ask the Spirit to guide your thoughts and emotions, then describe your situation in a sentence or two.

5. To write your own lament, follow David's structure from Psalm 13. Consider using concise phrases. Imagery and metaphors can help carry an emotion if you're having trouble putting it into words.

- Complaint … As you make your heart known to God, use the most honest language you can to describe your situation. God can handle and desires your strongest emotions.

- Petition … Ask God to act on your behalf. What is it that you most long for from Him? What do you need? What do you desire?

- Praise … Even in the midst of your suffering, what is the praise that you can offer to God? What is your heart toward Him? How do you choose to act in faith?

6. Read through your lament. Consider giving it a title.

7. If you're working through this exercise on your own, close by reading your lament aloud to God. If you're working through this exercise in a group, consider sharing your lament with the group, closing in prayer for each other.

FACING
YOUR IDOLS

[PSALM 23]

The familiarity of Psalm 23 can be a barrier when trying to engage it in a new way or a new season of life ... seeing past memories of it read at funerals, memorization of it as a kid, messages heard on it, books read about it. As I began to read through the psalm I asked God to help me see beyond my years of engaging this psalm. What is something new You have for me this morning?

What I felt stood out surprised me, "I shall not want." Right at the top of the psalm. I kept reading but couldn't get passed that phrase. As I began to turn that phrase over and over in my head thoughts came to mind of some of the good work around idols I've been doing recently. As we lead a discipleship intensive at our church we talk through the root idols we all face ... power, control, approval, and comfort. These are at work below the surface of our lives, they drive our motivations and desires. What we see birthed out of these root idols is the sin, or surface idols, that appear in our lives ... money, sex, greed, etc. We tend to look to these root idols for a full life instead of Jesus who is Life.

How are you seeking life apart from God? How are you trying to meet your needs outside of your relationship with Jesus? My desire is to respond as David did ... "The Lord is my shepherd; I shall not want."

"GOD IS GREAT
... SO I DON'T HAVE TO BE IN CONTROL.

GOD IS GLORIOUS
... SO I DON'T HAVE TO FEAR OTHERS.

GOD IS GOOD
... SO I DON'T HAVE TO LOOK ELSEWHERE
FOR MY SATISFACTION.

GOD IS GRACIOUS
... SO I DON'T HAVE TO PROVE MYSELF."

Tim Chester, *You Can Change*

[PSALM 23]

SPIRITUAL EXERCISE

---

1. Begin with a few minutes of silence and let your heart be still.

2. Read through Psalm 23, slowly.

3. Answer the following questions.
    • When do you feel most at peace?
    • What keeps you up at night?
    • What do you wake up thinking about?

4. Read through the chart on the following page and put a check by what feels most true about you ...

POWER IDOL

- HAS TO BE IN A POSITION OF POWER OR INFLUENCE
- DEMANDING, PEOPLE BECOME MEANS TO GET A TASK DONE
- VALUE IS FOUND IN HOW MUCH YOU GET DONE/PRODUCE
- OTHER PEOPLE'S WORTH IS IN WHAT THEY PRODUCE OR OFFER
- HAS BURSTS OF ANGER
- CRITICAL OF OTHERS, JUDGES EASILY

APPROVAL IDOL

- TAKES CRITICISM AND FAILURE BADLY
- FINDS IT HARD TO RELAX
- CONSTANTLY TRYING TO MANAGE HOW OTHERS VIEW THEM
- REPUTATION IS EVERYTHING, SELF-MADE, PROUD
- EASILY ENVIOUS OF OTHERS
- NEEDS TO BE INCLUDED AND CRAVES RECOGNITION

CONTROL IDOL

- CAN BE OVERBEARING, METICULOUS OVER SMALLEST OF THINGS
- IS INFLEXIBLE, RIGID, VERY PLANNED OUT
- ANY CHANGE LEAVES THIS PERSON ANXIOUS, ALMOST FROZEN
- CAN BE IMPATIENT WITH THEMSELVES AND OTHERS
- HAS TROUBLE ASKING FOR HELP OR BEING IN NEED OF OTHERS
- HIDES WEAKNESSES
- CONDEMNING OF OTHERS, SELF-RIGHTEOUS

COMFORT IDOL

- MINISTRY IS A BURDEN NOT A JOY
- OFTEN COMPLAINS
- MAKES PEOPLE FEEL A BURDEN OF DUTY
- LACKS JOY
- INCONSISTENT MOODS
- "ME" TIME IS GUARDED AT ALL COSTS

Chart adapted from *Gospel Coach*, Scott Thomas and Tom Wood

5. Answer the following questions.

   • Which of the four root idols do you most identify with?

   • What does this idol promise you?

   • What specific harm does this idol cause you and others?

6. Read back through your answers to the questions. How might Jesus, the True Shepherd, be what you're seeking most?

7. Is there anything you need to say to God? Is there anything you believe God might be saying to you?

8. Write out a prayer to God, naming the idols in your life, asking Him to help you let go of the idol and cling to Him for all you need.

9. If you're working through this exercise in a group, share what you feel comfortable sharing.

RE-WRITING AND
PRAYING A PSALM

→

[PSALM 35]

In Psalm 35 David calls out for God to fight for him, asking God to destroy his enemies. The amount of violence in the psalms is shocking at some level. I don't know that I would have survived those days. My enemies are much different. As I journaled before engaging Psalm 35, I didn't write anything about a shield or a battle-axe, that morning I was dealing with my familiar foe—financial worry and stress. I wrote, "I feel the weight on my chest, like I can't breathe." I tend to carry stress as a tightness in my chest. As I read, "Say to my soul, 'I am your salvation'!" I felt myself asking God for the same thing—for Him to remind my soul of who He is—trading the tightness in my chest for a lightness and deep breaths.

While our leadership spent a year working with consultants on new mission and vision for our church, one of the consultants, Will Mancini, talked about his growth in understanding the psalms. He described the psalms as, "The only book in the Bible of our words to God. They are God's Word to us about how to speak with Him. They are like a father teaching a child, 'this is how you speak to your mother.'" Using the psalms as a guide to learn to speak to God resonated with me.

When I got to the end of my prayer time, I sat quietly, not really sure what to do next. Sometimes I feel prompted to act, sometimes I just wait silently, then close my journal and move into the next part of my day. As I went back through the lines I'd written from the psalm that resonated with me, I began to re-write them in my own words. Then I simply prayed that prayer to God.

It was helpful for me to use David's words as a guide on how to speak with God about my struggle. As I journey through the Psalms, reading how the psalmists engage God from their depths and heights, I am learning to speak differently with God—more freely, honest, and vulnerable.

[PSALM 35]
SPIRITUAL EXERCISE

---

1. Begin with a few minutes of silence and let your heart be still.

2. Identify a challenge you're facing, or something that is consuming your thoughts or your emotions. Describe it as you write it down in a few sentences.

3. Pay attention to what you're feeling regarding your challenge and write down those emotions in a few sentences.

4. As you think about this challenge, what is the deep desire you're aware of?

5. Engage the Psalm. Read through Psalm 35, slowly. Take a few minutes to read back through it and write down a few lines or sentences that stand out to you—maybe one to three.

6. Read slowly through the few sentences you wrote down.

7. Now, write each of those sentences in your own words.

8. To close this time, use your own words as a prayer to God. If you're working with a group, encourage everyone to read their sentences aloud as a prayer. The leader may close when the group is finished.

9. As this conversation continues between you and God, one question to consider …

    What might God's invitation be to you in this place?

Any psalm will work with this exercise, but here are a few others to consider:

Psalm 28 - Hear My Plea for Mercy

Psalm 61 - Lead Me to the Rock

Psalm 46 - God Is Our Refuge and Strength

Psalm 62 - My Soul Waits for God Alone

Psalm 63 - Your Steadfast Love Is Better Than Life

Psalm 56 - When I Am Afraid I Put My Trust in You

YOUR NEED, GOD'S ACTION

⟶

[PSALM 54]

There is a structure to Psalm 54 that stood out as I read through it a few times. I see three parts to this psalm ...

1. What David needed.
2. How he desired God to act.
3. His posture in the waiting.

As with what seems to me like most of the Psalms, David is up against enemies that want to take his life. In my prayer time, I wrote that I felt pretty settled that day. I saw no "enemies" camped outside my office. I wasn't facing a tough day, relational strife, or leadership struggles. As I had journaled through the questions I usually answer, I'd written my desire for my prayer time, "I desire for You to meet me in Your Word."

Some mornings I feel like God's Word jumps out of the page and literally applies itself in my day without me doing much at all. Those days are not as common as I would hope. Many days I do my best to stay engaged in my prayer time as long as I feel led. But I do believe God answered my prayer that morning and prompted me to answer the question, "What do I need from God?" This led me to follow David's structure of the Psalm.

"DO NOT BE ANXIOUS ABOUT ANYTHING, BUT IN EVERYTHING BY PRAYER AND SUPPLICATION WITH THANKSGIVING LET YOUR REQUESTS BE MADE KNOWN TO GOD. AND THE PEACE OF GOD, WHICH SURPASSES ALL UNDERSTANDING, WILL GUARD YOUR HEARTS AND YOUR MINDS IN CHRIST JESUS." PHILIPPIANS 4:6-7

[PSALM 54]
SPIRITUAL EXERCISE

---

1. Begin with a few minutes of silence and let your heart be still.

2. Read through Psalm 54, slowly.

3. Discuss your observations from Psalm 54.
   - What did David need from God?
     (save me, vindicate, me, hear my prayer)
   - How did he desire God to act?
     (help me, sustain, destroy them)
   - What was David's posture?
     (sacrifice, give thanks, trust)

4. Applying this to your situation …
   - What do you need from God right now?
   - How do you desire God to act on your behalf?
     (if you need help, use the following I AM statements below to guide you)

5. One final question …
   - What is your posture toward God right now?

6. Close with a minute of silence, honoring God's work through His Spirit, then offer your prayer to God.

7. If you're working through this exercise in a group, share what you feel comfortable sharing.

I AM STATEMENTS:

"JESUS SAID TO THEM, 'I AM THE BREAD OF LIFE;
HE WHO COMES TO ME SHALL NOT HUNGER,
AND HE WHO BELIEVES IN ME SHALL NEVER THIRST.'"
JOHN 6:35

"AGAIN JESUS SPOKE TO THEM, SAYING, 'I AM THE LIGHT
OF THE WORLD. WHOEVER FOLLOWS ME WILL NOT WALK
IN DARKNESS, BUT WILL HAVE THE LIGHT OF LIFE.'"
JOHN 8:12

"I AM THE DOOR. IF ANYONE ENTERS BY ME, HE WILL BE
SAVED AND WILL GO IN AND OUT AND FIND PASTURE."
JOHN 10:9

"I AM THE GOOD SHEPHERD. THE GOOD SHEPHERD
LAYS DOWN HIS LIFE FOR THE SHEEP."
JOHN 10:11

"JESUS SAID TO HER, 'I AM THE RESURRECTION
AND THE LIFE. WHOEVER BELIEVES IN ME,
THOUGH HE DIE, YET SHALL HE LIVE,
AND EVERYONE WHO LIVES AND BELIEVES IN ME
SHALL NEVER DIE. DO YOU BELIEVE THIS?'"
JOHN 11:25-26

"JESUS SAID TO HIM, 'I AM THE WAY,
AND THE TRUTH, AND THE LIFE. NO ONE COMES
TO THE FATHER EXCEPT THROUGH ME.'"
JOHN 14:6

"ABIDE IN ME, AND I IN YOU. AS THE BRANCH CANNOT
BEAR FRUIT BY ITSELF, UNLESS IT ABIDES IN THE VINE,
NEITHER CAN YOU, UNLESS YOU ABIDE IN ME. I AM THE
VINE; YOU ARE THE BRANCHES. WHOEVER ABIDES IN ME
AND I IN HIM, HE IT IS THAT BEARS MUCH FRUIT,
FOR APART FROM ME YOU CAN DO NOTHING."
JOHN 15:4-5

INVITING JESUS
INTO YOUR REALITY

———————————————————————➤

[PSALM 55]

Psalm 55 is David's conversation with God after a friend has betrayed him. In the psalm David names his reality (vs. 1-3), he deeply feels his reality (vs. 4-15), invites God into it (vs. 16-19), then chooses how to live out of his reality (vs. 22-23).

The morning I spent time in Psalm 55 I wrote in my journal that I was trying not to "go south from two responses from two different conversations." I'd had a few difficult conversations with some people and wasn't sure where they would lead. Fear and anxiety were churning inside me. What resonated with me is David's sentence, "Attend to me and answer me; I am restless in my complaint and I moan." I was distracted by those two responses from people. What did they mean about me? Were more difficult conversations coming? Why is life so full of relational strife? We are complicated relational beings.

My old instinct would have been to think or act my way out of the anxiety. Instead, I began to engage David's work in my journal —naming my reality, feeling it deeply, inviting Jesus into it, and asking God what His invitation is to me in this place. It's the work I'd encourage you to embrace. You can't think or work your way from anxiety to trust. Begin by inviting Jesus into the midst of your anxiety and allow the Holy Spirit room to do His good work.

> **"ALL SHALL BE WELL, AND ALL SHALL BE WELL, AND ALL MANNER OF THINGS SHALL BE WELL."**
>
> *Julian of Norwich*

[PSALM 55]
SPIRITUAL EXERCISE

---

1. Begin with a few minutes of silence and let your heart be still.

2. Read through Psalm 55, slowly.

3. Take a few minutes and think about or discuss the following questions from the psalm ...
    • What is David's reality? (vs. 3, 12-14)
    • What is David feeling? (vs. 2, 4, 5)
    • What are David's desires? (vs. 6, 9, 15)
    • How does David choose to live out of his reality? (vs. 16, 22)

4. Let David's words be your guide as you answer the following questions ...
    • What is your reality right now? Maybe there's something in your life that's causing you anguish or grief. Maybe there's a challenge in front of you with leadership or relationships. Name your reality in a few sentences.
    • What emotions are you feeling? Feel that reality and capture the emotion in a few sentences.
    • What are your desires in this situation?
    • What do you most long for?

5. Take a few minutes in prayer to bring those thoughts, emotions, and desires to Jesus. Let Him fully know you and love you.

6. One final question …

    • How might you choose to live out of this reality?

7. Close your time with a minute of silence to honor the work of the Spirit, or offer your prayer to God.

8. If you're working through this exercise in a group, share what you feel comfortable sharing.

EMBRACING
A CHALLENGE

[PSALM 56]

The first ten years of my career were spent working in the marketplace. When I left that to take a full-time pastor position on staff with our church, I wasn't ready for how different full-time ministry can be. My wife and I used to laugh about me coming home tired. Wasn't I just having coffee with people?! Well, yes (and there was a whole lot of other work to do), and having coffee with people wore me out. Of course, it was much more than it sounds—being present in the moment, empathizing and sharing another's burden as they unpack their life, as they unload a painful memory or challenge they face. All of that does take mental and emotional energy, and it wears me out at times.

The morning I sat down with Psalm 56, I wrote the following … "I come today, bracing for a long day, a lot of meetings, emails piling up, things that have to get done—and the meetings and the people I'm meeting with need my presence. Today will take a lot of emotional and mental energy." I knew not all of my meetings or conversations that day were going to be simple or enjoyable. I had complaints coming at me from four different people—I felt surrounded.

As I looked ahead at my day and engaged Psalm 56, I was aware of so many phrases that resonated with how I was feeling, "be gracious to me, O God," "when I am afraid," "what can flesh do to me?" "put my tears in your bottle," and so on. As I sat silently in those words and breathed slowly, deeply, I became aware that in David's conversation with God, he talks about three things …

1. His challenge with the Philistines.
2. His relationship with God.
3. His request of God in His challenge.

I pray that as you name a challenge as David did, you would feel the soothing words of Psalm 56 lift your soul, and allow you to sit silently and breathe deeply. In this place, your challenge and fears and desires fully known by God, may you rest before our God, in whom we trust and shall not be afraid.

> **GOD OF LIFE,**
> THERE ARE DAYS WHEN THE
> BURDENS WE CARRY
> CHAFE OUR SHOULDERS
> AND WEAR US DOWN;
> WHEN THE ROAD SEEMS DREARY AND ENDLESS,
> THE SKIES GRAY AND THREATENING;
> WHEN OUR LIVES HAVE NO MUSIC IN THEM
> AND OUR HEARTS ARE LONELY,
> AND OUR SOULS HAVE LOST THEIR COURAGE.
> FLOOD THE PATH WITH LIGHT,
> **WE BESEECH YOU;**
> **TURN OUR EYES**
> **TO WHERE THE SKIES**
> **ARE FULL OF PROMISE.**

Augustine

[PSALM 56]

SPIRITUAL EXERCISE

---

1. Begin with a few minutes of silence and let your heart be still.

2. Read through Psalm 56, slowly.

3. Take the time to sort out the Psalm. Write out the words of the Psalm in the appropriate category.
    *   David's conversation with God about his challenge with the Philistines: (vs. 1-7)
    *   David's conversation with God about their relationship: (vs. 8-11)
    *   David's request of God in this challenge: (vs. 12-13)

4. In a few sentences, write out a challenge you're facing.

5. Using David's words as a guide, write out the following in your journal ...
    *   Tell God about your challenge.
    *   What's your posture toward God?
    *   What's His posture toward you?
    *   What do you need from God?

If you're struggling putting words around what you need from God, consider praying the following prayer for a person that is challenging, inserting their name in the prayer—or your insert your name in the prayer, requesting God's steadfast love, peace, joy, and freedom:

May (you) be filled with the steadfast love of God today,
May (you) have peace, May (you) be joyful,
And may (you) be free today in Christ. Amen.

6. If you're working through this exercise in a group, share what you feel comfortable sharing.

WAITING
ON GOD

→

[PSALM 62]

When David was writing Psalm 62 he was under attack. Men were threatening him, attempting to overthrow him as king, and trying to kill him. That's likely not going to happen to me, but when something is wrong with one of our children, I can feel as desperate. The morning I read Psalm 62 I was waiting on results from our son's appointment with a doctor. He's had a heart murmur since birth, it's never been anything serious, but he'd been complaining of some symptoms and his doctor decided we needed to check into it further. Even when the doctor says, "no cause for worry," I worry.

I'm a gifted worrier. I call worry and fear "the twins." They've been like a low-grade fever for me over the years, always present in some degree. God has worked with me on that in some significant ways throughout my life. Still, in moments like these I come face to face with worry and fear. I'm aware of the tendencies in me to fix things, to order and control, and yet there was nothing I could do ... nothing. In this moment, with the news pending, I sat ... waiting.

My mind wanted to take me to terrible places. I did my best to hold fast in the present moment with God. Reading through the psalm, two things stood out to me ... "My soul, wait in silence for God only," and "Pour out your heart before Him." I began to think through those two phrases. As I sat with God in the waiting, the silence, a few questions came to mind. I ended up with a heartfelt response to God, reminding myself of God's character, and the truth of His Word.

Our son was fine in the end. "No cause for worry." But what did God do in the waiting? He drew me closer in relationship to Him. He used this moment to reveal my tendencies to control, and to remind me of my total dependency on Him. And I think He used this moment to continue to shape me and transform my character to be more like Jesus. As you sit in the waiting, I pray He leads you to a place of trust and peace, and deeper relationship with Him.

 "GOD DESIRES OUR SEARCH AND OUR DESIRE. THROUGHOUT SCRIPTURE, REPRESENTATIVES OF THE HOLY ONE TELL US TO 'FEAR NOT' AND TO BE AT 'PEACE.' THE ANTITHESIS OF FEAR IS NOT CERTAINTY, BUT RATHER THE VITALITY OF RELATIONSHIP."

Susan S. Phillips, *Candlelight*

[PSALM 62]

SPIRITUAL EXERCISE

1. Begin with a few minutes of silence and let your heart be still.

2. Read through Psalm 62, slowly.

3. Four questions …
   - What is in your life that you've been waiting on God to answer, address, heal, redeem, direct, or deliver?
   - In the waiting, what is your most consistent thought or prayer?
   - What does it feel like to wait?
   - Where do you imagine God is in the waiting?
     (silent, loving, present, absent, etc.)

4. Read back through verses 5-8. David encourages us to "pour out our heart before God." Take time to share your heart with God … your feelings of anger, fear, worry, anxiety, gladness, sadness, trust … tell God how you feel as you write them down in your journal.

5. Read back through verses 11-12. David reminds himself and us that our God is a God of power and steadfast love. Power belongs to God so we don't have to look to ourselves or anywhere else. Not only is our God all-powerful, our God is full of steadfast love.

Describing David's use of the word, *hesed* (steadfast love), Charles Spurgeon writes in *Treasury of David*, "This tender attribute sweetens the grand thought of His power: the divine strength will not crush us, but will be used for our good; God is so full of mercy that it belongs to Him, as if all the mercy in the universe came from God, and still was claimed by Him as His possession."

6. Aware of the waiting, your thoughts and feelings, and with David's closing words of God's power and steadfast love, offer your prayer to God ... your desire of Him in this place of waiting (written or spoken aloud).

7. If you're working through this exercise in a group, share what you feel comfortable sharing.

YOUR RELATIONSHIP
METAPHOR

→

[PSALM 63]

Desperation. That's what I hear when I read through Psalm 63 … "earnestly I seek you," "my soul thirsts for you," "my flesh faints for you," "my soul clings to you." Am I desperate for God? Have I ever been absolutely desperate for God?

David wrote this psalm when he was in the wilderness, having fled from Absalom who led a rebellion against him. When I think of when I've been desperate for God it's usually around critical moments in my life … when my father was dying of cancer, when our first child was born premature and spent ten days in newborn intensive care, during a struggle with a difficult situation in our church, or I when was a wrestling a big decision in my life. But something else came to my mind that morning.

For a year, as part of my training in Spiritual Direction, I journeyed through the Ignatian Exercises. It was refreshing for me to experience a new way to engage the Bible. There was a rhythm, a path, and someone (a director I would meet with) to help me pay attention to the Spirit's work in my life. In the Ignatian Exercises you spend time in the Word contemplating God's love, your sin, then trace the life of Jesus from His birth, ministry, death, and resurrection. I was all in, following Jesus through the gospels for a year. God literally met me in His Word like never before. I felt like every day He would jump out of the pages with an application for that very day. I was "satisfied as with fat and rich food" … full and overflowing.

Then it ended. The exercises were over. I decided to keep going into the book of Acts, and then the wheels feel off. God seemed to disappear. I began to refer to that spiritual dryness as "post IEs." I would say that my relationship with God was like a desert ... a wilderness. I would drag myself from chapter to chapter in Acts without quenching my thirst or satisfying my hunger for God. It felt like I couldn't find my way back to the oasis that I had thrived in for a year or so. I felt like giving up. I feared the delight I'd finally found in God's Word was going to turn back into duty and responsibility.

I had a deep desire for relationship with God, a desperation coming out of the depths of who I am. I had looked upon God intently and experienced His power and glory in a new way. I longed for the kind of intimacy with God that I had tasted and seen. It was about a year and a half of that desert before I began to experience God in a similar way—alive, meeting me in His Word more often than not.

I hope this time in Psalm 63 and this exercise will open your heart to pay attention to where your relationship is with God right now, and I pray you are able to find God in how He is at work all around you, through you, and within you.

 METAPHORS HAVE TEETH. THEY KEEP US GROUNDED TO WHAT WE SEE RIGHT BEFORE US.

Eugene Peterson, *Practice Resurrection*

[PSALM 63]

SPIRITUAL EXERCISE

---

1. Begin with a few minutes of silence and let your heart be still.

2. Read through Psalm 63, slowly.

3. Take a few minutes to notice the structure of this psalm and journal any thoughts ...
   - David's deep desire for God (vs. 1-4)
   - David's joy in remembering his relationship with God (vs. 5-8)
   - David's faith that God will act on His behalf (vs. 9-11)

4. Answer the following questions ...
   - How are you experiencing God in relationship right now?
   - What do you long for in your relationship with God?

5. David uses the metaphors of "thirsting for God" (vs. 1) and "being satisfied as with a feast" (vs. 5) as he talks about his relationship with God. Think about how you could put words around your relationship with God and complete the following sentence. Don't worry about getting it perfect. Ask the Spirit to guide you, begin writing and let your thoughts flow.
   - My relationship with God right now is like ...

6. If you need to, read back through what you just wrote and clearly state it in a sentence.

7. More aware of where you are with God right now, what might His invitation be to you in this place?

8. Close your time with a minute of silence to honor the work of the Spirit, or offer your prayer to God. Consider closing your time with the Lord's Supper.

9. If you're working through this exercise in a group, share what you feel comfortable sharing. Consider closing your time with the Lord's Supper.

THE LORD'S SUPPER

When we participate in the Lord's Supper we look back, remembering Christ's sacrifice to bring us into relationship with God. In the present, we engage together in the physical act of eating the bread to remind us of His body broken, and drinking the cup to remind us of His blood shed for us. And we look to the future, when Christ will come again to make all things new. No more thirsting, fainting, or desperation for God. Instead, fullness of relationship … satisfaction … a glorious feast.

"The trajectory of human history was set at the cross, and it has been set to this one end: That the elect may feast forever in the presence of God. At the Lord's table, we receive an initial taste of the final heavens and earth, but the Lord's Supper is not merely a *sign* of the eschatological feast, as if the two were separate feasts.

Instead, the Supper is the early stage of that very feast. Every time we celebrate the Lord's Supper, we are displaying in history a glimpse of the end of history and anticipating in this world the order of the world to come." Peter Leithart, *Blessed are the Hungry.*

As we take the bread and the cup, let us be reminded of Jesus' words from John 6:35, "I am the bread of life; whoever comes to me shall not hunger, and whoever believes in me shall never thirst."

Take the elements together. "And when he had given thanks, he broke it, and said, 'This is my body, which is for you. Do this in remembrance of me.' In the same way he also took the cup, after supper, saying, 'This cup is the new covenant in my blood. Do this, as often as you drink it, in remembrance of me.' For as often as you eat this bread and drink the cup, you proclaim the Lord's death until he comes.'" 1 Corinthians 11:24-26

PRESENT MOMENT, HOLY MOMENT

[PSALM 84]

I spent a few years meeting with a Spiritual Director, someone who listens well and asks good questions, to help me pay attention to my relationship with God and respond to my awareness of God. I remember a certain meeting we had with me telling him what I saw as the edge of my growth. I was working hard to be present in each moment of the day ... and struggling. Honestly for me, it takes a lot of energy and attention. I told him that after I left the serenity and stillness of our meeting I'd be heading home where I knew what awaited me ... a full-on attack by my nine-year-old son. We'd be playing hard until bedtime. I had a lot on my mind, but my desire was to be present with him. It was a challenge for me to fully be in the moment.

As we ended our session he had me pay attention to my breathing. I've found that paying attention to my breathing helps me get out of my head and into the present—aware of myself physically in the moment. It also helps still my racing mind. As I breathed in he invited me to think "present moment," and as I breathed out "grateful moment." Then he encouraged me to pause before I got out of my car (to face the onslaught) and repeat that exercise. When I got home I did that, but I confused the wording. Instead I said to myself as I breathed in and out, "present moment, holy moment." I didn't realize this until later.

As I thought about that for a few days, and repeated the exercise, the truth of that phrase, "present moment, holy moment," began to resonate in me. Since the Holy Spirit is living in me, the more present I am in the moment to how He is at work in me and all around me, the more every moment can be a holy moment. Ever since, I find myself breathing in and out slowly with those words in mind ... "present moment, holy moment." They help me settle my anxious thoughts and turn my attention to my relationship with God.

When I read Psalm 84, the phrases that stood out to me were, "my soul longs, yes, faints for the courts of the Lord," and "for a day in your courts is better than a thousand elsewhere." That's what it feels like sometimes to me, sitting in God's presence fully in the moment, my spirit is satisfied. I really believe that a thousand days in the greatest place I could imagine doesn't compare to a day spent resting fully in God's presence.

There's a stanza from a poem, "Aurora Leigh" by Elizabeth Barrett Browning, that captures how I see the growth of my awareness and presence with God ...

> *Earth's crammed with heaven, and*
> *every common bush afire with God;*
> *But only he who sees, takes off his shoes.*
> *The rest sit round it and pluck blackberries.*

I feel like I was busy plucking blackberries for so many years, unaware that the bush was afire with God. I was busy doing something good, but I was missing what was deeper, more beautiful and holy. Not until I learned to be present with God did I begin to find Him in everything, truly take off my shoes, and be present in the moment with Him.

[PSALM 84]
SPIRITUAL EXERCISE

---

1. Begin with a few minutes of silence and let your heart be still.

2. Read through Psalm 84, slowly.

3. Re-read these three verses and follow the prompts for each ...
   "Blessed are those who dwell in your house." (vs. 4)
   - Describe what it's like for you to dwell in God's presence.

   "Blessed are those whose strength is in you." (vs. 5)
   - Thinking ahead on your day, what are some ways you might rely on your own strength rather than God's?

   "Blessed is the one who trusts in you." (vs. 12)
   - What is a tangible way you could put your trust in God today?

4. Take two minutes and sit silently before God. Pay attention to your breathing to help you stay in the present instead of following thoughts into your head. As you breathe in slowly, think "present moment," and as you breathe out think "holy moment."

5. "For a day in your courts is better than a thousand elsewhere." (vs. 10) Today can be "one day." Close this exercise with your own prayer asking God to give you strength and help you trust Him as you seek to spend this day in His presence.

Write out your prayer in your journal, or if you're by yourself consider speaking it aloud to God instead of talking with Him in your mind.

6. If you're working through this exercise in a group, you can close your group by discussing what stood out in the exercise, or by discussing what it's like for each person to dwell in God's presence.

ESTABLISH THE WORK
OF OUR HANDS

[PSALM 90]

Psalm 90 has always been one of my favorites ... the beautiful phrasing, the grandeur ... and as I've read, as far as we know it's the only psalm written by Moses. When I imagine all the miracles of God that Moses witnessed, and then he writes, "Let your work be shown to your servants, and your glorious power to their children. Let the favor of the Lord our God be upon us, and establish the work of our hands upon us; yes, establish the work of our hands!" I pay attention. He knows what he's talking about. He's seen God's glorious power ... the parting of the Red Sea, manna from heaven, water from a rock, the burning bush. I had someone ask me once if I'd considered what it must have been like for Moses the day after the burning bush. Hmm ...

What resonated with me as I read the psalm is the perspective of time Moses carries throughout ... "all generations," "everlasting to everlasting," "You return man to dust," "teach us to number our days," "establish the work of our hands." So many days I get busy quickly, without this perspective. I can have a narrow focus and lose sight of God's larger narrative at work—for me, my family, for His church, this world.

As I sat with the psalm I began to see a structure to it that led me to prayer ...

1. He is God (vs. 1-2)
2. I am not (vs. 3-11)
3. But He is with me (vs. 12-17)

I've mentioned before, but this past year brought a lot of changes to our organization—leadership structure, vision, new values and clarifying mission. I have been desperate for God to do what only He can do in that process. I also need that desperation each day. As I engaged the work in this exercise, I felt my shoulders relax, my hands open, and my eyes look upward as I honestly prayed for God's help.

I want today, and every day for me to be like I imagine it must have been for Moses the day after the burning bush. I want to look expectantly for God in the most surprising places, to see Him work and hear Him speak. I desire to see His glorious power, and for Him to establish the work of my hands.

[PSALM 90]
SPIRITUAL EXERCISE

---

1. Begin with a few minutes of silence and let your heart be still.

2. Read through Psalm 90, slowly.

3. Engage the three sections of the psalm:

   He is God ... "From everlasting to everlasting you are God."

   - List some of the ways you've seen God clearly working throughout your life.
   - Thinking of attributes of God (Omniscient, Omnipresent, etc.), how are you experiencing God today?

   I am not ... "You return man to dust."

   - How are you experiencing your own limitations, and your changing health—physically, mentally, emotionally?
   - What is before you right now that feels like "toil and trouble"?

   But He is with me ... "Let the favor of our Lord be upon us."

   - When you read verse 14, what deep desires surface?
   - What do you need from God right now?

4. As you close your prayer time this morning, do so as Moses does, with a prayer for God to establish the work of your hands. Mindful that "He is God, I am not, But He is with me," and

aware of what's going on within you, offer your day, your work as your worship to God. You could possibly use some of the following thoughts to guide you …

- Invite God into your most mundane tasks, asking for Him to help you see eternal purposes.
- Ask Him to help you find a balance between the relational needs of yourself and others and tasks that must get done.
- Ask Him to help you deepen your trust in Him and your thankfulness for His presence and leading.

5. If you're working through this exercise in a group, share what you feel comfortable sharing, and close together in prayer.

SWEPT UP IN CELEBRATION

[PSALM 98]

Psalm 98 screams celebration. As I read the psalm in my prayer time, the celebration burst out of the ink on the page, dramatic and poetic. "All the ends of the earth have seen the salvation of our God." Immediately I thought of Jesus and His saving work for me.

Once I see something Messianic in the psalms I pick up a book that's next to my chair written by my friend Nancy Guthrie, *Discovering Jesus in the Old Testament*. When I flipped through her book, she had titled an entry on Psalm 98, "Salvation Is Found in No One Else." She writes, "The Bible speaks of salvation in terms of the past, present, and future. There is a sense in which we *were saved* (from before the foundation of the world); we *were being saved* (by the work of God in history); we *are saved* (having been justified by faith); *we are being saved* (by being sanctified or made holy); and we *will be saved* (from the wrath to come). This salvation—past, present, and future—is completely God's doing. We can do nothing to save ourselves and we contribute nothing to our own salvation."

A friend once asked me, "Do you trust God with your spiritual growth?" I think when I'd gotten a taste of something deeper in my relationship with God I was doing all I could to dive in head first and force myself to grow. Can I trust that God is working to grow me and draw me into a deeper relationship with Him?

When I read back through the first three verses, I wrote down what God is doing …

- He has done marvelous things
- His right hand and His holy arm have worked salvation for Him
- He has made known His salvation
- He has revealed His righteousness in the sight of the nations
- He has remembered His steadfast love and faithfulness

Of course I can trust He who began a good work in me to bring it to completion. As I read back through verses 4-9, they felt like one layer of praise after another. The thought occurred to me, there is not only salvation past, present, and future, but celebration past, present, and future. I can join the celebration that has been going on in heaven before the foundation of the world, throughout history, now in the present, and most certainly in the future—for eternity. That's where the Spirit led me that morning, swept up in the celebration … "Oh sing to the Lord a new song, for He has done marvelous things!"

[PSALM 98]
SPIRITUAL EXERCISE

1. Begin with a few minutes of silence and let your heart be still.

2. Read through Psalm 98, slowly, then ...
   - Write down what thoughts come to mind as you read the psalm? What stood out to you? Why?
   - Write down what emotions come to the surface as you read the psalm? What are you feeling?

3. Read through verses 1-3 again, then spend some time reading through the following, contemplating the saving work of God past, present, and future ...

before the foundations of the world ...
"Blessed be the God and Father of our Lord Jesus Christ, who has blessed us in Christ with every spiritual blessing in the heavenly places, even as he chose us in him before the foundation of the world, that we should be holy and blameless before him." Ephesians 1:3-4

throughout history ...
"Now the Lord said to Abram, 'Go from your country and your kindred and your father's house to the land that I will show you. And I will make of you a great nation, and I will bless you and make your name great, so that you will be a blessing. I will bless those who bless you, and him who dishonors you I will curse, and in you all the families of the earth shall be blessed." Genesis 12:1-3

"Your way, O God, is holy. What god is great like our God? You are the God who works wonders; you have made known your might among the peoples. You with your arm redeemed your people, the children of Jacob and Joseph. … Your way was through the sea, your path through the great waters; yet your footprints were unseen. You led your people like a flock by the hand of Moses and Aaron." Psalm 77:13-15; 19-20

fully justified in Jesus …

"But God shows his love for us in that while we were still sinners, Christ died for us." Romans 5:8

"In him we have redemption through his blood, the forgiveness of our trespasses, according to the riches of his grace, which he lavished upon us, in all wisdom and insight making known to us the mystery of his will, according to his purpose, which he set forth in Christ as a plan for the fullness of time, to unite all things in him, things in heaven and things on earth." Ephesians 1:7-10

sanctified by the work of the Spirit …

"Now may the God of peace himself sanctify you completely, and may your whole spirit and soul and body be kept blameless at the coming of our Lord Jesus Christ. He who calls you is faithful; he will surely do it." 1 Thessalonians 5:23-24

"And I am sure of this, that he who began a good work in you will bring it to completion at the day of Jesus Christ." Philippians 1:6

complete in Christ's return to make all things new ...

"And to wait for his Son from heaven, whom he raised from the dead, Jesus who delivers us from the wrath to come."
1 Thessalonians 1:10

"'He will wipe away every tear from their eyes, and death shall be no more, neither shall there be mourning, nor crying, nor pain anymore, for the former things have passed away.' And he who was seated on the throne said, 'Behold, I am making all things new.'"
Revelation 21:4-5

4. What emotions and deep desires stir in you? Write those down.

5. Read through verses 4-9 again and imagine the anthem of praise growing with each verse. Allow yourself to be swept up in the celebration. How would you like to respond to God and join the celebration throughout history, now in the present, and for all eternity?

6. If you're working through this exercise in a group, share what you feel comfortable sharing. You might get creative with how you close your time ... a corporate prayer of praise, or a song of praise. I will offer this benediction that came to my mind as I finished my prayer time. The pastor at my home church would speak it over the congregation most Sundays to close our worship service. It reminded me of God's providence and faithfulness, saving work and ongoing sanctification.

"

**DEPART NOW IN THE
FELLOWSHIP OF GOD THE FATHER.
AND AS YOU GO, REMEMBER,
IN THE GOODNESS OF GOD
YOU WERE BORN INTO THIS WORLD.
BY THE GRACE OF GOD,
YOU HAVE BEEN KEPT ALL THE DAY LONG,
EVEN UNTO THIS VERY HOUR.
BY THE LOVE OF GOD,
FULLY REVEALED IN THE FACE OF JESUS,
YOU ARE BEING REDEEMED.**

"

John R. Claypool

RULER OVER
EVERYTHING

→

[PSALM 99]

I never know how I will experience God when I sit down to spend time with Him. Sometimes I read through the Scripture, re-reading, working hard to engage with it in my life, but I might not get as far as I'd hoped. Sometimes I get interrupted, and many times I end and realize it was just a good time spent reading and praying. Sometimes though, I feel God leaps off the page and speaks directly into my day.

When I sat down with Psalm 99 I started by writing how I come to my prayer time. I knew that what I'd been up in the night thinking about needed to come out. I'd had a significant meeting the previous day that I was really excited about. I left, however, angry with the results (or lack of results), and even angry with the way I'd engaged others in the meeting. I wrote several questions, and tried my best to answer them …

- What is my deep desire underneath these feelings?
- How is my root idol expressing itself?
- What am I afraid of?

When I read through Psalm 99 slowly, I wrote down the phrase, "Ruler over Everything." Verses one though five leave no room for anything else … "let the peoples tremble," "He sits enthroned upon the cherubim," "you have executed justice and righteousness," "holy is he!" I wrote down a few more descriptive words as I thought of the phrase, "Ruler over Everything." Then I sat in silence for a few minutes because I didn't know where to go from there. I thought my time might be over, as it sometimes ends that way. In the silence I felt the question, "But is He ruler over everything?" Then, "What needs to come under His authority?"

[PSALM 99]

SPIRITUAL EXERCISE

---

1. Begin with a few minutes of silence and let your heart be still.

2. Read through Psalm 99, slowly.

3. Read back through verses 1-5 and meditate on those words.

4. Write down some words and thoughts that come to mind as you think of God, enthroned above, as ruler over everything. Then, answer the next questions.
   • How might you be trying to take that authority from Him?
   • What needs to come under His authority?

5. What is the posture of your heart toward God?

6. How would you demonstrate that with your body? (write it down, draw it out, or move physically to demonstrate it)

7. Express the posture of your heart toward God in a prayer to Him.

8. Close with a minute of silence, honoring God's work through His Spirit.

9. If you're working through this exercise in a group, share what you feel comfortable sharing.

REMEMBERING THE MOMENT

[PSALM 100]

I love Psalm 100. It feels like a celebration. I shake my head a bit, because I'm not big on celebrations. If I'm honest, when I think about a celebration the first thoughts that come to mind are—this is going to take a lot of planning, it will be crowded with people, way too loud, and there will be a lot of mess to clean up once it's over. It makes me sad that those are my honest, initial thoughts. That speaks a bit to my unhealthy default—we've got to do this right, I don't care for uncertainty, and spontaneity is costly. That's been an edge of my growth that I have had to press into. I have to choose to be present in the moment and enjoy it. Embrace the experience. Choose joy. Celebrate.

Writing that makes me think of a celebration I loved. When my oldest son graduated from high school we invited the people that had spoken into his life over for a dinner—his two small group leaders and their wives, two other young leaders at church, a few men and their wives he'd served with at church, a teacher from high school, our neighbors, a family that had supported him significantly. It did take a lot of planning. There was a mess to clean up. There were a lot of people in our home, and it was noisy. But I'll never forget it. I crafted the words I wanted to say to thank each of those people. In that moment we celebrated my son and the people in his life who mattered.

My sister tells a story of sitting next to my grandmother, Elisabeth, as she was in her final days. She wasn't very coherent—

wasn't aware of us, her condition, where she was. At one point she said, "Well, there's Harold!" (her husband, my grandfather). She named a few other people as if they were lining up to greet her. I imagine the veil between this life and the life to come was becoming more and more transparent. Kind of joking and a bit excited, my sister asked, "Do you see Bob Howard?" (our father). If it truly was heaven she was beginning to get a glimpse of, for sure my father would be there lining up. But the truth is, he would probably be last to get in line. He embraced the moment. People. The joy and celebration. He brought the energy into a room like lightning. My sister is like that too. But I do hope heaven is like that—people lined up to greet us as we enter. "Have you heard who's coming?!" "Hurry up, get in line!" "Elisabeth, we've been waiting to see you!" I want to be a part of that kind of celebration—crowds, noise, and all.

The exercise that follows is based on an exercise I learned in my Spiritual Direction training. It helps us remember a moment or experience that stands out to us—it could be a celebration, it could even be a difficult experience or memory—unpack it a bit, hold it before God, and maybe get some greater understanding of its significance. It could be used as a way to catch up after a season apart, or as a way to share more deeply with each other. We'll anchor this exercise in Psalm 100, capturing the joy and celebration, and the assurance, that in whatever moment we remember we have a God who made us, calls us His own, is the One who leads us, cares for us, provides for us, and whose love will never end, faithful forever, throughout every generation.

[PSALM 100]
SPIRITUAL EXERCISE

---

1. Begin with a few minutes of silence and let your heart be still.

2. Read through Psalm 100, slowly.

3. Unpack Psalm 100 briefly together. There are two sections (verses 1-2 and 4) that call us to praise, rejoice, and give thanks to God. Then two sections (verse 3 and 5) that remind us who God is: our Creator, our Father, our Shepherd who cares for us and leads us, He is good, His steadfast love will not end, and His faithfulness is forever.

4. Write a paragraph or two describing a recent significant experience. It could be a celebration or even a challenging moment.

5. Three steps ...
   • Read ... Read your paragraph slowly, once, then again, slowly, and notice what word(s) or phrase stands out to you. Write it down.

   • Listen ... What is it about that word or phrase that makes it stand out to you? Hold it before God. Write down your thoughts.

- Respond … As you begin to discern why that stood out to you, how would you respond to God? Write down your response.

6. Read through Psalm 100 one more time, slowly.

7. Close with a minute of silence, honoring God's work through His Spirit, then offer a prayer of thanksgiving to God.

WHOLEHEARTED
REPENTANCE

→

[PSALM 103]

In an average week I spend about four or five days in my morning time with God. Some mornings I start earlier than usual, some days I just can't wake up on time ... I've learned to give myself grace and look forward to the days when I carve out the time and get to sit with God.

As I engaged Psalm 103 it had been a few days for me ... early meetings and crowded days hadn't allowed the usual time. But as I sat in silence to start my time, I realized something that had become apparent over the past few days ... I came face to face with some sin in my life and didn't want to think about it ... I wanted to run and hide.

Reading through Psalm 103, I was undone by David's poetic phrase, "For he knows our frame; he remembers that we are dust." Why does that line always bring me to my knees? I think I'm overwhelmed by God's great compassion for me. My Creator remembers.

Here's what I wrote in my journal ...

"For he knows our frame; he remembers that we are dust."

A call to praise ... "Bless the Lord, O my soul, and all that is within me, bless His holy name!"

How God acts … He forgives us, heals us, redeems us, crowns us with His love and mercy, and He satisfies us.

Who God is … merciful, gracious, slow to anger, abounding in steadfast love, just, compassionate, and understanding.

Who I am … like the grass, flourish for a moment, then the next I am gone.

So then … "Bless the Lord, O my soul!"

As we've worked with the four areas of the heart (in the Psalm 8 exercise) and walked through the pathway from thoughts, emotions, desires, to choices, this exercise takes a choice we've made and walks us through the pathway in reverse. This helps us be more aware of what was going on within us as we made the choice—what was under the surface, driving our action. It's a pathway to repentance, engaging our whole heart.

> "BUT THE MAN WHO IS NOT AFRAID TO ADMIT EVERYTHING THAT HE SEES TO BE WRONG WITH HIMSELF, AND YET RECOGNIZES THAT HE MAY BE THE OBJECT OF GOD'S LOVE PRECISELY BECAUSE OF HIS SHORTCOMINGS, CAN BEGIN TO BE SINCERE. HIS SINCERITY IS BASED ON CONFIDENCE, NOT IN HIS OWN ILLUSIONS ABOUT HIMSELF, BUT IN THE ENDLESS, UNFAILING MERCY OF GOD."
>
> Thomas Merton, *No Man Is an Island*

[PSALM 103]
SPIRITUAL EXERCISE

1. Begin with a few minutes of silence and let your heart be still.

2. Read through Psalm 103, slowly.

3. Unpack the psalm briefly, using the sections listed above. Write down in your journal "How God Acts ..." and "Who God Is ..." and fill out those lists with David's words from the psalm.

4. Think of a recent sin in your life and write it out in a few sentences—maybe it's how you reacted or acted out, what you used as a means of escape, how you interacted with someone else, disobedience to God.

5. Journal your answers to these three questions ...
   • What was I longing for in choosing that sin?
   • What emotion was I feeling when I made that choice?
   • What was I thinking that led me to that action?

6. Aware of all that was going on within you as you chose that sin, what would you like to say to God? Write that down in your journal.

7. As David encourages us to bless the Lord with all that is within us ... write a prayer of praise to God in your journal.

8. If you're working through this exercise in a group, share what you feel comfortable sharing.

CULTIVATING GRATITUDE

→

[PSALM 105]

I love to create lists, check off the items and feel the satisfaction of getting things done. Before I began reading Psalm 105, I created a pretty robust "list" as I answered the question, "How do I come to this prayer time?" There were a few transitions ahead at work that I was worried about. I'm really aware of my daughter's upcoming transition to college and all that will accompany that—great sadness, excitement for her, fear, a desire for her to experience God in it. There were a few other family-related items on my list that I was curious about but trying not to overthink them. When I finished and read back through the list, I felt the weight on my chest—the stress—it was just heavy. I moved on to write what I desire from God in this time, "I desire for God to help me satisfy my soul."

As I read Psalm 105 I wrote down the phrase that stood out to me, "Remember the wondrous works that he has done." I read through the litany of works that God did for Israel, and when I got to the end it seemed abrupt. I expected more of a refrain at the end and all that was there was, "Praise the Lord!" I went back to my journal and circled "Remember the wondrous works he has done," then wrote at the very bottom of my page, "Praise the Lord!" I then set out to create another list and fill in that blank space with the works I've seen God do in my life.

The first few I wrote were the biggies—those moments when God showed up in dramatic ways. As I kept writing my thoughts settled into those things right around me. It was sweet to remember. It truly turned my heart to one thing … praise. As I began to praise God and thank Him for His faithfulness to me, it did something within me … a weight lifted, the tension I was carrying was released, and my soul felt satisfied. I was able to take those worries I was carrying into my prayer time and lay them at Jesus' feet, trusting my faithful God to be in control in each situation. As you cultivate gratitude in this exercise, I pray your heart opens to praise and your hands open to trust.

"IF THE ONLY PRAYER YOU SAID WAS 'THANK YOU,' THAT WOULD BE ENOUGH."
Meister Eckhart

[PSALM 105]
SPIRITUAL EXERCISE

1. Begin with a few minutes of silence and let your heart be still.

2. Write down how you come to this time ...
   • What are you thinking about?
   • What are you feeling?
   • What are you longing for?

3. Read through Psalm 105, slowly.

4. At the top of the page in your journal write the phrase, "Remember the wondrous works that he has done..." At the bottom of your journal write, "Praise the Lord!"

5. Now spend some time thinking about and writing down how you've seen God at work in your life. It could be your own salvation, could be how you've seen Him in your family's life, your children's life, big moments and small moments. Ask the Spirit to lead you.

6. When you're finished, pray a prayer of gratitude for the list you just wrote, naming each item as you pray. "I praise You, Lord for ..."

7. Before you're done, go back to what you wrote about how you come to this prayer time. Is anything there that you're holding too tightly? Is there a worry or fear that you could release to God? What might you need to trust God for? If so, talk to God about that for a few minutes.

8. If you're working through this exercise in a group, take time now to share briefly about the works you've seen God do, and what it is you need to trust Him for.

ADDING YOUR
VERSE

[PSALM 107]

The structure of Psalm 107 is very poetic ... or even song-like with verses and a chorus. I was very aware of this as I was reading through it, so I began to put a bracket around the "verses" in my Bible (vs. 4-7, 10-14, 17-20, 23-30, 33-42), and then the "choruses" (vs. 8-9, 15-16, 21-22, 31-32). The psalmist even uses a bit of an intro and outro as well. As I read through the psalm a few times, I felt the invitation to add my verse to the song. In the intro the psalmist encourages us to, "Let the redeemed of the Lord say so," and in the outro, "Whoever is wise, let him attend to these things." What would I say about my salvation? How has God rescued me? How is He growing me? How has God recently revealed to me His power and glory? What is one verse that I could add?

I spent time that morning writing my verse ... how I'd seen God recently at work in my life through situations and people, leading me by His Spirit to grow in ways I couldn't have understood a year or so ago. When I finished, I added the chorus to my verse (personalizing it a bit), "Thank You Lord for Your steadfast love and wondrous works in my life, Your child! I will praise You."

[PSALM 107]

SPIRITUAL EXERCISE

---

1. Begin with a few minutes of silence and let your heart be still.

2. Read through Psalm 107, slowly.

3. Take the time to mark the different parts of the song ...
    - Intro (vs. 1-3)
    - Verse 1 (vs. 4-7)
    - Chorus (vs. 8-9)
    - Verse 2 (vs. 10-14)
    - Chorus (vs. 15-16)
    - Verse 3 (vs. 17-20)
    - Chorus (vs. 21-22)
    - Verse 4 (vs. 23-30)
    - Chorus (vs. 31-32)
    - Verse 5 (vs. 34-42)
    - Outro (vs. 43)

4. Spend a few minutes thinking about the verse you'll write. Is it your salvation experience? Is it a recent encounter with God? It could be a dramatic intervention when God rescued or healed. Ask the Spirit to guide you, then write your verse when you are ready.

5. Once you've completed your verse, add the chorus, "Let them thank the Lord for his steadfast love, for his wondrous works to the children of man!" Notice that each chorus the psalmist adds one more phrase after the first. Take the time now to personalize your chorus and write it down.

6. If you're working in your personal prayer time, close by reading back through Psalm 107, adding your verse and chorus to the end. If you're working with a group, have the leader read the intro (vs. 1-3) then let everyone take turns reading their verse and chorus, with the leader closing the time by reading the outro (vs. 43).

RESPONDING TO SALVATION

[PSALM 116]

When I read through Psalm 116, I didn't expect to contemplate my salvation. As usual, I wrote down how I come to this prayer time—my emotions, thoughts—then what I desire from God during this time. The phrases that stood out to me were ... "I love the Lord, because he has heard my voice and my pleas for mercy," "For you have delivered ... my eyes from tears," and then, "Precious in the sight of the Lord is the death of his saints."

I spent some time thinking about that last phrase. I remember hearing it used at funerals. I like the idea that God would love us so much that our death would be precious to Him. Not until I read a bit more about the word "precious," did I think of that word as more than "dearly loved." As I read about how that word is translated, I understood a greater depth in the verse ... that God looks upon our death as "costly and of great value" ... like a precious jewel.

That thought led me to the great price that God paid for us, for our salvation in the life, death and resurrection of Jesus. A love so great, our life and death of such value, that He would pay the greatest price, the death of His only Son.

Like the psalmist, I found the words of worship and thanksgiving coming from my heart, "I love the Lord, because he has heard my voice and pleas for mercy." "Gracious is the Lord, and righteous; our God is merciful. The Lord preserves the simple; when I was brought low, he saved me." May you also respond in worship and thanksgiving to your salvation in Jesus, or even respond for the first time in confessing and believing that Jesus is Lord and Savior.

[PSALM 116]
SPIRITUAL EXERCISE

---

1. Begin with a few minutes of silence and let your heart be still.

2. As you read through Psalm 116 slowly, notice the psalmist is responding in worship to God's act of salvation. Write down any phrase or word that stands out to you.

3. Re-read verse 15. Spend some time thinking about the word "precious" and it's meaning not only of "dearly loved" but of "costly and of great value." When you think about God calling your death "costly and of great value," write down the thoughts and emotions that surface in you.

4. Slowly read through the following verses, contemplating your salvation ...
    *   1 Timothy 1:15, "The saying is trustworthy and deserving of full acceptance, that Christ Jesus came into the world to save sinners, of whom I am the foremost."
    *   2 Corinthians 5:21, "For our sake he made him to be sin who knew no sin, so that in him we might become the righteousness of God."
    *   John 3:16-18, "For God so loved the world, that he gave his only Son, that whoever believes in him should not perish but have eternal life. For God did not send his Son into the world to condemn the world, but in order that the world might be saved through him. Whoever believes in him is not condemned, but whoever does not believe is

condemned already, because he has not believed in the name of the only Son of God."

- Romans 10:9-10, "If you confess with your mouth that Jesus is Lord and believe in your heart that God raised him from the dead, you will be saved. For with the heart one believes and is justified, and with the mouth one confesses and is saved."
- Romans 10:13, "For everyone who calls on the name of the Lord will be saved."
- Romans 8:38-39, "For I am sure that neither death nor life, nor angels nor rulers, nor things present nor things to come, nor powers, nor height nor depth, nor anything else in all creation, will be able to separate us from the love of God in Christ Jesus our Lord."

5. As you remember the price that was paid by Jesus for your own salvation, because God looks upon you as precious—costly and of great value—how would you like to respond to God? (If you haven't believed that Jesus is Lord and asked Him to save you, why not? What is holding you back? What might His invitation be to you right now?)

6. If you're working through this exercise in a group, take time now to share briefly about your salvation and your response to God.

A WHOLEHEARTED
APPROACH TO A PSALM

[PSALM 121]

Excited and Tired. That's a familiar refrain for me. Those two words sum up my last year and a half and they show up regularly in my journal as I ask myself the question, "How do I come to this prayer time?" This morning was no different. I wrote, "I come to this time excited for new opportunities in my role to use my creativity—grateful for new vision and direction—tired from all the effort in the transition."

As I engaged Psalm 121 that morning, the idea of "wholehearted" kept surfacing in my mind. I've mentioned before that "wholehearted" is our thoughts, emotions, desires, and choices—bringing all of who we are to Jesus for transformation and fullness of life. For most of my life I lived a "behavior modification" type of approach to my faith. What am I learning? How can I apply it? That's great, but I've realized it is only half of the equation. What do I do with these emotions and deep desires within me? How do I invite Jesus into the midst of those deep, dark places to help me see more clearly what's going on in me? How can He help me understand the motivations that might be driving my choices and actions?

I used my thoughts, emotions, desires, and choices—in that order—to guide my morning prayer time. I invite you to engage your time the way I engaged mine and try a wholehearted approach to Psalm 121.

[PSALM 121]
SPIRITUAL EXERCISE

---

1. Begin with a few minutes of silence and let your heart be still.

2. Two questions to answer before engaging the Word ...
   • How do you come to this prayer time? "I come today ..."
   • What do you desire from God during this time? "I desire ..."

3. Read Psalm 121 slowly, allowing the words to not just engage your mind, but sink deeply into your soul. Read through Psalm 121 again, slowly.

4. Pray, asking the Holy Spirit to be your guide as you walk this pathway through the psalm, bringing to light what God has for you this morning.

5. Three questions to spend some time on, and answer based on your reading of Psalm 121 ...
   • As you read this psalm, what thoughts come to mind?
   • What feelings surfaced within you?
   • What deep desires does this psalm stir in you?

6. More aware of what's going on within you, read back through Psalm 121, slowly.

7. Pray, asking the Holy Spirit to lead you as you answer this final question ...

   • What choice do you need to make?

8. Sit quietly for a minute or two with God, not trying to move too quickly to an end. Be aware of what surfaces in your heart, and respond.

9. Pray to close your time as you feel led.

10. If you're working through this exercise in a group, share what you feel comfortable sharing.

IF THE LORD HAD NOT
BEEN ON OUR SIDE

[PSALM 124]

I think a lot about my life in reverse—how one step led to another, preparing me for the next, how God worked out a situation in a way I couldn't imagine—doing my best to trace His good hand at work in my life. It's definitely easier to see on the other side of a situation, down the road a bit farther.

As I read Psalm 124 in my morning prayer time, I engaged the story of the Israelites as they said, "If it had not been the Lord who was on our side." God was faithful to keep His people throughout their history, specifically as He delivered them from Egypt ... the ten plagues, their departure, the pursuit by Pharaoh's army, the parting of the Red Sea and their salvation.

God has been faithful to keep me throughout my life. I think of decisions I made in my immaturity of high school and college. I remember tragedies I faced, moments of seeking discernment at difficult crossroads, or following through on a decision to leave a place that was comfortable to step into the unknown. My life has not been without pain and suffering. It all didn't work out according to my plan. I'm glad it didn't. God has used all of those moments—the wonderful and the difficult—to draw me closer in relationship with Him, and to shape me to be more like Christ. If the Lord had not been on my side ...

I love classical music, for many reasons. One reason is that I see it as a fitting metaphor for life. A theme begins, it's brand new, it's beautiful, the melody twists and turns as we get to know it and fall in love with it. Then the composer begins to develop the theme. New harmonies are introduced and we're ushered into a new key. We are still aware of the theme, but things have changed. Then dissonance arrives and we begin to feel the tension. It doesn't seem as beautiful as it once was. We long for the purity and simplicity of the theme. These new notes and tonal shifts are spinning and spinning out of control and we're not sure if or when it will ever resolve. But resolution does come. Our shoulders relax, and the tightness in our chest and shoulders dissipates. Then our hearts begin to soar as we hear the theme again. It's the same but because of our experience—the new harmonies and the dissonance, the tension and release—it is far more grand. The beauty is richer, felt more deeply, known at a level that couldn't be understood or even imagined when we first heard the theme.

I think that's the way life is with our Composer, the Creator of heaven and earth. He is on our side—with us and won't leave us—working all things for our good. He allows us to experience sorrows and trials, joy and celebration, tension and release—His presence so tangible and intimate, and then distant, bringing seasons of dryness and loneliness. And through the soaring, the suffering, and the struggle, He is shaping us and growing us to be beautiful works of art for His glory.

> **PSALM 124 IS AN INSTANCE OF A PERSON WHO DIGS DEEPLY INTO THE TROUBLE AND FINDS THERE THE PRESENCE OF THE GOD WHO IS ON OUR SIDE. IN THE DETAILS OF THE CONFLICT, THE MAJESTIC GREATNESS OF GOD BECOMES REVEALED IN THE MINUTENESS OF A PERSONAL HISTORY.**

Eugene Peterson, *A Long Obedience in the Same Direction*

[PSALM 124]
SPIRITUAL EXERCISE

1. Begin with a few minutes of silence and let your heart be still.

2. Read through Psalm 124, slowly.

3. Write the first part of the psalm in your journal, personalizing it … "If it had not been the Lord who was on my side …"
   - Looking back through your life, think of one time or list many times that you've seen God work on your behalf.
   - Unpack the idea that God is on your side. What does that feel like? What has it meant for you that God is on your side? Do you feel that He has been on your side?

4. Write the next part of the psalm in your journal … "Blessed be the Lord …"
   - Write out your blessing to God. Who is He to you? What are the characteristics of God that have been so clear to you in these times?

5. Read slowly through what you've written. Close your time the way the Israelites closed their psalm, with the reminder that "Our help is in the name of the Lord, who made heaven and earth." What would you like to say to your Creator and Sustainer?

6. If you're working through this exercise in a group, share what you feel comfortable sharing.

LONGING FOR HEAVEN

[PSALM 126]

A question has been rattling around in my head for a little over two weeks ... "How do I long for heaven?" It first came to mind as we were in a discipleship group talking about Colossians 3:1-4 ...

"If then you have been raised with Christ,
seek the things that are above, where Christ is,
seated at the right hand of God.
Set your minds on things that are above,
not on things that are on earth.
For you have died, and your life is hidden with Christ in God.
When Christ who is your life appears,
then you also will appear with him in glory."

I wrote the question in the margin of my journal and listed a few bullet points of how I long for heaven ... I want things "right" and I long for perfection—I have a strong desire to "fix" broken things, there are relationships I miss that are now "on the other side," the longing for no more pain, sorrow, tears, fear, anxiety.

In Psalm 126 this morning my mind went back to that thought as I read, "we were like those who dream," "brought back the captive ones," "our mouth was filled with laughter and our tongue with joyful shouting." The psalm finishes with imagery of sowing the seeds and coming home with shouts of joy, reminding me of Jesus' command to go and make disciples. I went to several study Bibles to try and understand it better.

The psalm describes a time when Israel was rescued from captivity and restored to where they belong. The experience was so surprising and unexpected that it seemed like it was a dream. In the Faithlife Study Bible they unpacked verse 1, "brought back the captive ones," and the Hebrew word shivah. "The expression essentially indicates that Yahweh is returning something to the way it was before the calamity happened." Sounds like the work of Christ on our behalf, and sounds like heaven to me.

Another verse that I've been mindful of for several weeks is Colossians 1:13-14 …

"He has delivered us from the
domain of darkness and transferred us
to the kingdom of his beloved Son,
in whom we have redemption, the forgiveness of sins."

Because of the death and resurrection of Jesus, we have been rescued from darkness and sin, and transferred to His kingdom. And when Jesus comes again to complete His work, He will make all things new. Revelation 21:1-5 …

"Then I saw a new heaven and a new earth, for the first heaven
and the first earth had passed away, and the sea was no more.
And I saw the holy city, new Jerusalem, coming down out of heaven
from God, prepared as a bride adorned for her husband. And I heard a loud
voice from the throne saying, 'Behold, the dwelling place of God is with man.
He will dwell with them, and they will be his people, and God himself will
be with them as their God. He will wipe away every tear from their eyes, and
death shall be no more, neither shall there be mourning, nor crying, nor pain
anymore, for the former things have passed away.' And he who was seated
on the throne said, 'Behold, I am making all things new.'

That sounds like a dream to me ... laughter, joy, and shouting. I do long for heaven, for God to return us to the way it was before the calamity happened ... before the fall. A garden. God's dwelling place with man. Unbroken relationship. The constant pull of sin removed.

"For now we see in a mirror dimly,
but then face to face.
Now I know in part;
then I shall know fully,
even as I have been fully known."

1 Corinthians 13:12

[PSALM 126]

SPIRITUAL EXERCISE

1. Begin with a few minutes of silence and let your heart be still.

2. Read through Psalm 126, slowly.

3. Write the words or phrases from Psalm 126 that resonate within you and remind you of heaven.

4. What feelings surface as you think of heaven?

5. How do you long for heaven?
   How are those longings manifested in your life?

6. What choices might God be leading you to make based on your thoughts, feelings, and longings for heaven?

7. Gather those thoughts, feelings, longings, and choices and express them in a written or spoken prayer to God.

8. If you're working through this exercise in a group, share what you feel comfortable sharing.

OUT OF THE DEPTHS

[PSALM 130]

This day feels like a reprieve from the several days that surround it. I wrote in my journal that I feel "restful and settled" as I come to this prayer time. Usually it's "tired, anxious, excited," or "a bit numb." I then wrote that I desired God to "settle in with me this morning." The idea of feeling restful and settled, and the opening line from Psalm 130, "Out of the depths I cry to you, O Lord," reminded me of a poem I'd recently rediscovered. I was looking for something in an old journal and came across a poem my grandfather wrote. I'd recopied it in my journal a few years ago as it spoke to where I was at the time. It's called "Release."

My heart is freed for just a while
To slip the tug of earthly sight
And lures that softer thoughts beguile
Are cleansing all the world tonight

The baser things have lost their power
Dread hates and fears I do not see
To stretch the length of this sweet hour
Dear God, please linger yet with me

Grant I may keep this clear, pure joy
And sweet release that long I've sought
Nor let my wayward mind's alloy
E'er ruin the gold this hour has brought

- Reverend H.M. Hunt, 1955

When I asked my mom about the poem, she thought he wrote it during a tough season, struggling with depression—although they probably wouldn't have called it that back then. As a pastor, he dealt with many difficult situations and people. He pastored the church I grew up in for 25 years. I wish he were around to talk to. I'd like to talk to him about my experiences in ministry. I'd like to ask him about the deeper meaning of this poem … his fears, to explain the "sweet release," and to tell me more about the gold from that hour of lingering with God.

As I sat with Psalm 130 this morning, what resonated with me was "in his word I hope," and "plentiful redemption." Those two phrases felt like a deep breath—a "sweet release" to me. As I sat quietly with them, I began to catch a broader view of the psalm. I see it in four parts:

1. Naming your reality (vs. 1-2)
2. Confession (vs. 3-4)
3. Hope (vs. 5-6)
4. Assurance (vs. 7-8)

As you work this exercise, whether you're in the depths or walking in an extended time of sweet release, I pray you'll bring all of what you're feeling to God and find the gold in this hour of lingering with Him.

[PSALM 130]
SPIRITUAL EXERCISE

1. Begin with a few minutes of silence and let your heart be still.

2. Read through Psalm 130, slowly. Notice the four parts to psalm …
   - Name your reality (vs. 1-2)
   - Confession (vs. 3-4)
   - Hope (vs. 5-6)
   - Assurance (vs. 7-8)

3. Spend time answering the following questions in your journal. Ask the Holy Spirit to lead you.

   "Out of the depths I cry to you, O Lord!"
   - What do you wake up thinking about?
   - What are you praying most regularly about?
   - How would you describe your relationship with God today?

   "But with you there is forgiveness."
   - What is going on in your life that you need to confess to God?
   - Complete this sentence … Lord, I feel _____ as I admit that _____.

"I wait for the Lord, my soul waits, and in his word I hope."

• When you are fearful or discouraged, where do you turn?

• What does it mean to "hope in His Word"?

"For with the Lord there is steadfast love, and with him is plentiful redemption."

• How are you experiencing God's steadfast love
  (His faithful, loyal love)?

• If not, what would you like to ask or say to God?

• What Scriptures about hope give you assurance?

4. Close by offering a prayer to God based on your above answers.

5. If you're working through this exercise in a group, share what you feel comfortable sharing.

CONTENT IN HIS PRESENCE ALONE

[PSALM 131]

I've been in a season—a longer season—of change, struggle, and hard work. With all the challenges that surround me, I'm very aware of one more difficult conversation or email, one more head appearing in my doorway with a quick question, one more mistake to fix in my side project or piece of the production to juggle, and one more day marked off before graduation.

This morning I struggled with the question, "How do I come to this prayer time?" I sat quietly for a while. I worked through my thoughts, emotions, and desires. I finally ended with, "I hope today is a relaxing day. I don't really feel excited or tired, settled, at ease. I feel a bit like interruptions will happen and I'll have to fix them." I unpacked a few more emotions around a situation and moved onto the next question, "What do I desire from God during this time?" I wrote, "I desire for God to speak through His Word and for His presence to be felt." Then I began to engage Psalm 131.

I noticed three parts to David's psalm ...

1. Humility (vs. 1)
2. Contentment (vs. 2)
3. Hope (vs. 3)

As I engaged the first verse of the psalm, to walk humbly, I thought about what I seek and the root idols we discussed with Psalm 23. Do I seek approval, control, power, comfort? Am I more aware of a humble spirit or a prideful spirit?

In the second and third verse of the psalm, I became a little more aware of what life the past several months has felt like for me. I'll say concisely what took me about thirty minutes to process … I've been looking for contentment in my circumstances, not in God's presence and my hope in Him.

As I said earlier in the book, I wrestle with the root idol of control. Things can seem okay if there's enough money in the bank, my inbox is empty, no fires are burning, and everything is in its proper place. I'm content … in my circumstances.

David talks about the weaned child that can rest in his mother's lap and be content with his mother's presence alone. In an online message from John Piper ("Join Me in Soul-Satisfaction in God") he writes, "The weaned child is simply enjoying the way it feels to be in the lap of his mother. He is satisfied. And it is not about his stomach. It's about his heart. This is a picture of David's restfulness, contentment, satisfaction, joy, peace in the secure, loving presence of God."

That was what my soul desired this morning as I sat down for my prayer time … God's presence, felt. Contentment in my circumstances is temporary. Contentment in God's presence is eternal. I desire to walk humbly, learn contentment, and live in hope … to continue growing in my awareness of what's going on within me, and find my soul satisfied only by the presence of God.

> **"OUR HEARTS ARE RESTLESS, GOD, UNTIL WE FIND OUR REST IN THEE."**
> Augustine

[PSALM 131]

SPIRITUAL EXERCISE

---

1. Begin with a few minutes of silence and let your heart be still.

2. Two questions to answer before engaging the Word ...
    *   How do you come to this prayer time? "I come today ..."
    *   What do you desire from God during this time? "I desire ..."

3. Read through Psalm 131, slowly. Notice the three parts to psalm ...
    *   Humility (vs. 1)
    *   Contentment (vs. 2)
    *   Hope (vs. 3)

4. **Humility** ...
    *   In what areas of your life are you most likely to struggle with humility?
    *   Do you find yourself more focused on controlling things around you, longing for comfort and pleasure, a desire for recognition and power, or a longing for the approval and praise of others?

5. **Contentment** ...
   - Is your soul more quieted and satisfied, or anxious and discontent? Why do you think that is the case?
   - Are your actions marked more by a peaceful trust and a cheerful spirit, or an irritated churning and thoughts of comparing? Explain more about that.

6. **Hope** ...
   - Is hope manifested in your actions more through self-reliance or confidence in God?
   - What are you aware of in your life right now that makes you most long for hope?

7. **Invitation** ...
   - Read back through your answers to those questions.
   - With a short prayer, ask the Spirit to meet you where you are and lead you to rest in God's presence. Spend some time in silence.
   - How might God be inviting you to walk humbly, learn contentment, and live in hope?

8. Close by writing or speaking aloud your prayer to God.

9. If you're working through this exercise in a group, share what you feel comfortable sharing.

GOD'S FAITHFUL, LOYAL LOVE

[PSALM 136]

Psalm 136 shouts, "for his steadfast love endures forever." And as I read through it that's what stood out to me … obviously, you can't miss it! When I see "steadfast love" or hesed, I've learned to pay attention. I've heard it referred to as one of the most important words in the Bible. God's hesed is His faithful, loyal love for His people. I went back to the Spiritual Exercise from Psalm 62 for the Charles Spurgeon quote from *Treasury of David* I'd read describing God's hesed …

"THIS TENDER ATTRIBUTE SWEETENS THE GRAND THOUGHT OF HIS POWER: THE DIVINE STRENGTH WILL NOT CRUSH US, BUT WILL BE USED FOR OUR GOOD; GOD IS SO FULL OF MERCY THAT IT BELONGS TO HIM, AS IF ALL THE MERCY IN THE UNIVERSE CAME FROM GOD, AND STILL WAS CLAIMED BY HIM AS HIS POSSESSION."

God's merciful, faithful, gracious, promise keeping loyal love for His people. God is a covenant-making and covenant-keeping God. God's love for us is His covenant faithful love. In a short online article, "The Godward Focus of Faithfulness," John Piper writes about the foundation for God's hesed, "Here is how Jeremiah pleads for God's covenant-keeping mercy: 'Do not spurn us, for your name's sake; do not dishonor your glorious throne; remember and do not break your covenant with us.' (Jeremiah 14:21) Beneath covenant-keeping there is a more ultimate foundation: God's allegiance to his name—God's jealousy for the honor of the glory of his throne." Faithful, merciful, gracious, loyal, loving … it is who God is, always will be, forever.

I can imagine that as the Israelites would sing of God's covenant-keeping love and recount creation, their rescue from Egypt, and God delivering them to the Promised Land, at the front of their minds would be the covenants of God … with Abraham, Noah, David, and others. As I read it this morning, I was aware of the new covenant in Jesus, the true son of Abraham, perfect rescuer from sin, the true David, the Son of God, the complete sacrifice who alone can offer us forgiveness of sin. I sat quietly for a while, then began to respond as the psalmist exhorts, and I encourage you to respond as well … in giving thanks.

[PSALM 136]
SPIRITUAL EXERCISE

1. Begin with a few minutes of silence and let your heart be still.

2. Read through Psalm 136, slowly. Allow the refrain of "for his steadfast love endures forever" wash over you. I encourage you not to skip over it, even after several times of reading it.

3. Read verses 1-3. They affirm God's supreme authority—God of gods and Lord of lords. They encourage us to give thanks because God is good. Take a few minutes to respond to these verses in your journal. How you've seen God as good recently, or in moments throughout your life? When you finish, write the refrain at the end, "for his steadfast love endures forever."

4. Read verses 4-9. They remind us that our good God is Creator. He created this world, each of us and is committed to His creation. Take a few minutes to respond to these verses in your journal. Express your feelings about our world … it's beauty, the joy you find in it, even your sadness or anger about the fallenness of the world God created. When you finish, write the refrain at the end, "for his steadfast love endures forever."

5. Read verses 10-16. They retell the story of the Exodus, how God brought Israel out of slavery in Egypt, through the Red Sea, leading them through the wilderness. Take a few minutes to respond to these verses in your journal. What trial

or suffering has God brought you through? Let Him know what's in your heart as you recall that memory. When you finish, write the refrain at the end, "for his steadfast love endures forever."

6. Read verses 17-22. They retell how God brought His people, Israel, into the Promised Land. God was faithful to what He told Israel He would do. Take a few minutes to respond to these verses in your journal. How has God been faithful to you? How do you need God to be faithful right now? When you finish, write the refrain at the end, "for his steadfast love endures forever."

7. Read verses 23-26. Scholars believe the psalm turns to a more recent event in these final verses. I saw a possible parallel to the three stories above, kind of a summary to close ... "remembered us in our low estate," rescue from Egypt ... "rescued us from our foes," defeating the mighty kings and delivering their land ... "gives food to all flesh," our Creator who is over all. The psalmist closes with how he began, encouraging us to give thanks. Read back through your journal writing from this exercise, then write out your prayer of thanks for how you've seen God's steadfast love in your life. When you finish, write the refrain one more time at the end, "for his steadfast love endures forever."

8. Close by observing a few minutes of silence. If you're working through this exercise in a group, share what you feel comfortable sharing.

FINDING GOD
IN ALL THINGS

→

[PSALM 138]

We have a God who is personal, present, and overflowing with compassion for us. As I read through Psalm 138, 2 Corinthians 1:3-5 came to mind, "Blessed be the God and Father of our Lord Jesus Christ, the Father of mercies and God of all comfort, who comforts us in all our affliction, so that we may be able to comfort those who are in any affliction, with the comfort with which we ourselves are comforted by God. For as we share abundantly in Christ's sufferings, so through Christ we share abundantly in comfort too."

When reading through the psalms I've found it helpful to have a few study Bibles available. I came across this opening statement about the Psalm 138 in the *ESV Global Study Bible*, "This psalm offers thanks to God for signs of his constant care."

The thought of God's constant care reminded me of The Examen, a prayerful reflection on each day. It's an exercise that Ignatius developed and practiced daily. As I spent time during my study of Spiritual Direction, I practiced The Examen frequently. One gift in it for me was the opportunity to bring those moments to God that I wished would have been different—something I said, choices I made—that my inner critic would love to remind me of over and over. I learned to bring those moments to God, lay myself before Him, and receive His mercy, forgiveness, and grace. As I practiced this exercise, I became so mindful of the phrase, "finding God in all things." This idea is at the core of The Examen, and the core of Ignatian spirituality. The more we find God in all things—

awareness and presence—the more we can respond in thanksgiving to how we see Him at work in us, through us, and all around us. We can respond like David in Psalm 138, "I give you thanks, with my whole heart."

The following exercise is adapted from The Examen. I encourage you to allow the Holy Spirit to guide you through your day, to be more and more aware of God's constant presence and constant care, responding to Him in thanksgiving with your whole heart.

[PSALM 138]
SPIRITUAL EXERCISE

1. Begin with a few minutes of silence and let your heart be still.

2. Read through Psalm 138, slowly. Notice the many phrases that speak to God's constant care. Write down what resonates with you.

3. As you sit quietly, ask the Spirit to guide as you reflect on your day, remembering the moments you experienced. Write down what stands out to you.

4. Reading back through the moment(s) that stood out to you, what feelings and desires are you aware of?

5. Holding the moment(s) before God, what would you like to say to Him about it?

6. Looking toward tomorrow, mindful of God's presence and care for you today, offer a prayer of thanksgiving to Him for the gifts He offered in this time.

7. Close by observing a few minutes of silence. If you're working through this exercise in a group, share what you feel comfortable sharing.

DEEP KNOWING OF GOD, DEEP KNOWING OF SELF

[PSALM 139]

The idea that God knows me more intimately than I know myself, and that to know more of myself is to know more of God, has led to some significant growth for me over the past seven years. There are several quotes I love that are all saying the same thing …

"Lord, let me know myself; let me know you."
Augustine

"Nearly all the wisdom which we possess,
that is to say, true and sound wisdom,
consists of two parts:
the knowledge of God and of ourselves.
But, while joined by many bonds,
which one precedes and brings forth
the other is not easy to discern."
John Calvin, *Institutes of the Christian Religion*

"We do not find our true self by seeking it.
Rather, we find it by seeking God."
Dr. David Benner, *The Gift of Being Yourself*

"There is only one problem on
which all my existence,
my peace, and my happiness depend:
to discover myself in discovering God.
If I find Him I will find myself
and if I find my true self I will find Him."
Thomas Merton, *New Seeds of Contemplation*

I've heard this referred to as the "double knowledge," knowing God and knowing ourselves. The deep knowing of God and the deep knowing of self develop together. David talks about this deep knowing in Psalm 139. He knows that God has searched him and known him … "when I sit down and when I rise up," "my path and my lying down," "even before a word is on my tongue." Our Creator who, "knitted me together in my mother's womb," knows us better than we know ourselves, and He can help us know our true selves.

As I've grown in understanding a face to face relationship with God … bringing my most honest self to Him … I've experienced so much more of God, and so much more of who I am. I believe this is David's posture in the prayer that closes Psalm 139, "Search me, O God, and know my heart! Try me and know my thoughts! And see if there be any grievous way in me, and lead me in the way everlasting!" A deep desire to know and confess the darkness in us, the hidden sins, and the shame, and allow the light of God's grace to help us see more clearly who we are as children of God.

An exercise I learned from my instructor while studying Spiritual Direction is called the Location Exercise. Like a map in the mall, it helps you see where you are in relation to God. It is comforting to me that the exercise is anchored in Psalm 139. We don't have to find God. He is always present with us … "If I take the wings of the morning and dwell in the uttermost parts of the sea, even there your hand shall lead me, and your right hand shall hold me."

Where are you right now in relation to God?

[PSALM 139]
SPIRITUAL EXERCISE

1. Begin with a few minutes of silence and let your heart be still.

2. Read through Psalm 139:1-6, slowly.

3. As you sit quietly, ask the Spirit to guide as you answer the
    following questions:
    - In this season of life, what are my dominant thoughts?
    - In this season of life, what are my dominant feelings?
    - In this season of life, what are my dominant desires?
    - In this season of life, how is my body?
      (tired, energized, achy, etc.)
    - In this season of life, how would I describe my relationships?

4. Slowly read over your list twice. Notice the themes and write
    them down.

5. Two more questions:
    - In a sentence, where am I? "I am in a place of …"
    - What might be God's invitation to me in this place?

6. Read through Psalm 139:1-6 again. Close in prayer.

7. If you're working through this exercise in a group, share what
    you feel comfortable sharing.

PRAYING
YOUR CALENDAR

→

[PSALM 143]

Often my day begins with my prayer time—anywhere from 20 minutes to an hour journaling, reading the Word, praying— then I get to work—almost like I step from one realm into another. I have to catch myself, remind myself of my dependence on God— through prayer, stillness—or I can go through my day, grinding to get all the work done on my own.

In Psalm 143 David is writing from a place of upheaval. The enemy is pursuing him, he's come to the end of his resources, "his spirit faints within him," "answer me quickly," "hide not your face from me." His cries are out of deep desperation. My days usually begin in a leather chair, with air conditioning and espresso, yet I desire the same desperation for God—for my soul to thirst for God like a parched land.

This morning, verse 8 stood out to me, "Let me hear in the morning of your steadfast love, for in you I trust. Make me know the way I should go, for to you I lift up my soul." I desire to start everyday with the truth of God's Word, the reminder of His steadfast love for me …

"But now thus says the Lord, he who created you,
O Jacob, he who formed you, O Israel:
'Fear not, for I have redeemed you;
I have called you by name, you are mine.'"
Isaiah 43:1

"In this the love of God was
made manifest among us,
that God sent his only Son into the world,
so that we might live through him. In this is love,
not that we have loved God
but that he loved us and sent his Son to be
the propitiation for our sins."
1 John 4:9-10

I desire to start everyday putting my trust in God, with the willingness and desire for Him to lead me ...

"And the Lord will guide you continually
and satisfy your desire in scorched places
and make your bones strong;
and you shall be like a watered garden,
like a spring of water, whose waters do not fail."
Isaiah 58:11

"I will instruct you and teach you
in the way you should go;
I will counsel you with my eye upon you"
Psalm 32:8

As I sat with these thoughts in my mind, I began to think through my day. I had a long meeting on the agenda that I was unsure about—it was going to be a challenge. I had another meeting where I truly wanted to be present and be "like a spring of water" to someone. The idea to "pray my calendar" came to my mind, praying that God would lead me throughout my day, that I would so be aware of Him, desperate for Him, and that He would make me know the way I should go.

[PSALM 143]

SPIRITUAL EXERCISE

1. Begin with a few minutes of silence and let your heart be still.

2. Read through Psalm 143, slowly.

3. Spend some time with verses 5 & 6 … "I remember the days of old; I meditate on all that you have done; I ponder the work of your hands. I stretch out my hands to you; my soul thirsts for you like a parched land."
   - What are some memories of how you've experienced God?
   - How does your soul thirst for God?

4. Re-read verse 8 … "Let me hear in the morning of your steadfast love, for in you I trust. Make me know the way I should go, for to you I lift up my soul."
   - How have you experienced God's steadfast love for you?

5. Take out your calendar, or think through your day and list out what is before you. Pray through each moment of your day, asking God …
   - To make His way known to you
   - To increase your awareness of Him
   - To guide your thoughts, words, and actions
   - To help you open your hands to His will

6. Close by observing a few minutes of silence. You might physically take a posture of openness to God during this time.

7. If you're working through this exercise in a group, share what you feel comfortable sharing.

PRAISING GOD
THROUGH POETRY

[PSALM 150]

Coming to the end of my time in Psalms is bittersweet. I love finishing things—a good day at work, mowing the yard, checking off the list—rewarded with completion. Even with the sense of satisfaction, I feel sadness that it's over. This journey through the psalms has been going on for the better part of a year. I've experienced God in fresh new ways, I've worked through significant challenges, and the Holy Spirit has been leading and growing me through it all. I will miss my prayer time in the psalms as I turn my focus somewhere else in the Bible. And I know I'll be back in a year or two. The way I experience God in the psalms is unlike any other book of the Bible.

These last several psalms have been a strong crescendo to the end of the book. Psalm 145, 146, and 147 listing numerous ways God is active and engaged in our world and our lives. Then Psalm 148, 149, and 150 feel like wave after wave after wave of praise stirring me to respond. I want to create something beautiful, write a song, add my voice to the psalmist's invitation, "Let everything that has breath praise the Lord!"

I've written songs, but have always wanted to be a writer— a writer writer, like a novelist or a poet. Books are one of the loves of my life. I remember hearing Billy Collins read his poetry live in New York and was fascinated by how he could gather his thoughts and cleverly and powerfully deliver them with a dryness that was endearing.

I've tried my hand at poetry and it's always read like something I would've created in elementary school. But I wanted to try it again. I thought I'd better use guardrails, like a young bowler (and it was good that I had them). I researched different poetry types and decided to take a run at a Diamante poem. It is a poem of seven lines, that when finished makes the shape of a diamond.

I encourage you to add your voice to the cacophony of praise that concludes the psalms. Try something different. Praise Him for who He is and how you've seen Him at work, by praising Him through poetry.

[PSALM 150]
SPIRITUAL EXERCISE

1. Begin with a few minutes of silence and let your heart be still.

2. Read through Psalm 150, slowly. If you have time, read Psalm 148-150.

3. Take as long as you need to write your poem (might be 5-10 minutes). Remember to write it in a way with your spacing that creates the "diamond." ...

    Line 1 – Noun (subject) ... I suggest starting with "God" the subject of our praise, or one of His names that means something special to you.

    Line 2 – Two adjectives describing Line 1.

    Line 3 – Three "-ing" words describing Line 1.

    Line 4 – Four words ... two about Line 1, then two about a synonym of Line 1 (another name for God, with attributes that are meaningful to you)

    Line 5 – Three "-ing" words about this synonym (other name of God)

    Line 6 – Two adjectives describing this synonym (other name of God)

    Line 7 – Synonym (other name for God) for Line 1

4. Close by observing a few minutes of silence.

5.   If you're working through this exercise alone, read your poem aloud to God as a prayer. If you're working through this exercise in a group, enter a time of prayer, encouraging each member to read their poem as a prayer to God.

GATHERING
THE GRACES

[PSALM 118]

When I spent my year in the Ignatian Exercises, the director that lead me through them used the book *The Ignatian Adventure* by Kevin O'Brien. At the end of the experience he had a chapter titled "Gathering the Graces." His challenge in the exercise was to, "Remember in gratitude God's generosity to you, and acknowledge your own generous cooperation with grace."

I was reminded of this driving with my daughter the other day. We were coming home from a two-day trip, registering for her first semester of college courses. We were listing out all the good things that had happened in those two days to help her feel more comfortable entering college. The list was long. I was grateful for God's kindness, and how we were seeing Him at work.

I hope that through several of these exercises in Psalms you've seen God at work in your life, growing and leading you, and deepening your relationship as you sat face to face with Him. I encourage you to take your prayer time to go back through your journal, review different exercises, and gather a few significant moments to hold before God with gratitude for His grace.

[PSALM 118]
SPIRITUAL EXERCISE

1. Begin with a few minutes of silence and let your heart be still.

2. Two questions to answer as you begin your time with God ...
   • How do you come to this prayer time? "I come today ..."
   • What do you desire from God during this time?
     "I desire ..."

3. Review your journal and mark a few of the most significant times of growth or moments of experiencing God. Ask the Holy Spirit to guide you.

4. Summarize each experience you marked in the exercise with a statement.

5. For each statement, answer a few questions ...
   • How did you experience God's presence?
   • What strong desire does this make you aware of?
   • Who was God to you during this time?
   • Who were you to God during this time?
   • How might God be leading you to live because of this experience?

6. Read through Psalm 118, slowly.

7. Hold each moment before God in prayer with gratitude, even those that might have been difficult or painful, recognizing God's good hand at work. I encourage you to frame your prayer of gratitude like the psalmist in Psalm 118. Begin by reading verse 1, followed by your statements, closing with verses 28 and 29.

8. If you're working through this exercise in a group, allow each member to read their prayer of gratitude aloud.

Made in the USA
Las Vegas, NV
05 June 2022